C000093885

Sentences selected out of Solomon's Proverbs, and Ecclesiastes. English and Latin. In English by H. D. And since made Latin by S. Perkins, ... Improved with numerical indexes ... With two indexes: ... By Peter Selby, ...

ECCO

PRINT EDITIONS

Sentences selected out of Solomon's Proverbs, and Ecclesiastes. English and Latin. In English by H. D. And since made Latin by S. Perkins, ... Improved with numerical indexes ... With two indexes: ... By Peter Selby, ...

Multiple Contributors, See Notes
ESTCID: T092069
Reproduction from British Library
H. D. = Henry Danvers. Selected verses in the Authorised version. Parallel English and Latin texts. In this edition the words "numerical references" are in italics ad there is a colon after "indexes".
London : printed for A. Bettesworth: and J. Batley, 1728.
[12],167,[1]p. ; 12°

Eighteenth Century
Collections Online
Print Editions

Gale ECCO Print Editions

Relive history with *Eighteenth Century Collections Online*, now available in print for the independent historian and collector. This series includes the most significant English-language and foreign-language works printed in Great Britain during the eighteenth century, and is organized in seven different subject areas including literature and language; medicine, science, and technology; and religion and philosophy. The collection also includes thousands of important works from the Americas.

The eighteenth century has been called "The Age of Enlightenment." It was a period of rapid advance in print culture and publishing, in world exploration, and in the rapid growth of science and technology – all of which had a profound impact on the political and cultural landscape. At the end of the century the American Revolution, French Revolution and Industrial Revolution, perhaps three of the most significant events in modern history, set in motion developments that eventually dominated world political, economic, and social life.

In a groundbreaking effort, Gale initiated a revolution of its own: digitization of epic proportions to preserve these invaluable works in the largest online archive of its kind. Contributions from major world libraries constitute over 175,000 original printed works. Scanned images of the actual pages, rather than transcriptions, recreate the works *as they first appeared.*

Now for the first time, these high-quality digital scans of original works are available via print-on-demand, making them readily accessible to libraries, students, independent scholars, and readers of all ages.

For our initial release we have created seven robust collections to form one the world's most comprehensive catalogs of 18th century works.

Initial Gale ECCO Print Editions collections include:

History and Geography
Rich in titles on English life and social history, this collection spans the world as it was known to eighteenth-century historians and explorers. Titles include a wealth of travel accounts and diaries, histories of nations from throughout the world, and maps and charts of a world that was still being discovered. Students of the War of American Independence will find fascinating accounts from the British side of conflict.

Social Science

Delve into what it was like to live during the eighteenth century by reading the first-hand accounts of everyday people, including city dwellers and farmers, businessmen and bankers, artisans and merchants, artists and their patrons, politicians and their constituents. Original texts make the American, French, and Industrial revolutions vividly contemporary.

Medicine, Science and Technology

Medical theory and practice of the 1700s developed rapidly, as is evidenced by the extensive collection, which includes descriptions of diseases, their conditions, and treatments. Books on science and technology, agriculture, military technology, natural philosophy, even cookbooks, are all contained here.

Literature and Language

Western literary study flows out of eighteenth-century works by Alexander Pope, Daniel Defoe, Henry Fielding, Frances Burney, Denis Diderot, Johann Gottfried Herder, Johann Wolfgang von Goethe, and others. Experience the birth of the modern novel, or compare the development of language using dictionaries and grammar discourses.

Religion and Philosophy

The Age of Enlightenment profoundly enriched religious and philosophical understanding and continues to influence present-day thinking. Works collected here include masterpieces by David Hume, Immanuel Kant, and Jean-Jacques Rousseau, as well as religious sermons and moral debates on the issues of the day, such as the slave trade. The Age of Reason saw conflict between Protestantism and Catholicism transformed into one between faith and logic -- a debate that continues in the twenty-first century.

Law and Reference

This collection reveals the history of English common law and Empire law in a vastly changing world of British expansion. Dominating the legal field is the *Commentaries of the Law of England* by Sir William Blackstone, which first appeared in 1765. Reference works such as almanacs and catalogues continue to educate us by revealing the day-to-day workings of society.

Fine Arts

The eighteenth-century fascination with Greek and Roman antiquity followed the systematic excavation of the ruins at Pompeii and Herculaneum in southern Italy; and after 1750 a neoclassical style dominated all artistic fields. The titles here trace developments in mostly English-language works on painting, sculpture, architecture, music, theater, and other disciplines. Instructional works on musical instruments, catalogs of art objects, comic operas, and more are also included.

The BiblioLife Network

This project was made possible in part by the BiblioLife Network (BLN), a project aimed at addressing some of the huge challenges facing book preservationists around the world. The BLN includes libraries, library networks, archives, subject matter experts, online communities and library service providers. We believe every book ever published should be available as a high-quality print reproduction; printed on-demand anywhere in the world. This insures the ongoing accessibility of the content and helps generate sustainable revenue for the libraries and organizations that work to preserve these important materials.

The following book is in the "public domain" and represents an authentic reproduction of the text as printed by the original publisher. While we have attempted to accurately maintain the integrity of the original work, there are sometimes problems with the original work or the micro-film from which the books were digitized. This can result in minor errors in reproduction. Possible imperfections include missing and blurred pages, poor pictures, markings and other reproduction issues beyond our control. Because this work is culturally important, we have made it available as part of our commitment to protecting, preserving, and promoting the world's literature.

GUIDE TO FOLD-OUTS MAPS and OVERSIZED IMAGES

The book you are reading was digitized from microfilm captured over the past thirty to forty years. Years after the creation of the original microfilm, the book was converted to digital files and made available in an online database.

In an online database, page images do not need to conform to the size restrictions found in a printed book. When converting these images back into a printed bound book, the page sizes are standardized in ways that maintain the detail of the original. For large images, such as fold-out maps, the original page image is split into two or more pages

Guidelines used to determine how to split the page image follows:

• Some images are split vertically; large images require vertical and horizontal splits.
• For horizontal splits, the content is split left to right.
• For vertical splits, the content is split from top to bottom.
• For both vertical and horizontal splits, the image is processed from top left to bottom right.

3/5 X 15

SENTENCES

Selected out of

Solomon's PROVERBS,

And ECCLESIASTES.

ENGLISH and *LATIN.*

In *English* by H. D.

And since made *Latin* by S. *Perkins,*
late School-Master of *Christ-Hospital.*

Improved with *Numerical References*
to the *Rules* of SYNTAX used in the
Latin Version.

With Two INDEXES:
The *First,* As a GRAMMAR:
The *Second,* As a DICTIONARY
to the Whole.

By *PETER SELBY,* M. A. Master
of the *Grammar-School* in CHRIST-
HOSPITAL.

LONDON;
Printed for A BETTESWORTH, at the
Red-Lyon: And J. BATLEY, at the *Dove,*
both in *Pater-Noster Row,* 1728.

Advertisements.

BOOKS *Printed, and Sold by* ARTHUR BETTESWORTH, *at the* Red-Lyon. *And* J BATLEY, *at the* Dove, *both in* Pater-Nofter-Row.

Lately Publifh'd, (being Approv'd of by the moft Eminent School Mafters,)

THE Second Edition of Æfop's Fables in Englifh and Latin, Interlineary, for the Benefit of thofe who not having a Mafter, would learn either of thefe Tongues, with Sculptures. By John Locke, Gent price 3 s 6 d

Cornelius Nepos, price 3 s. 6 d

Eutropius, price 2 s 6 d.

Erafmus, price 1 s. 6d.

Corderius price 1 s

With Englifh Tranflations as literal as poffible, defigned for Beginners in the Latin Toague By John Clarke, Mafter of the Publick Grammar-School in Hull.

The London Vocabulary, Englifh and Latin, put into a New Method proper to acquaint the Learner with Things, as well as pure Latin Words, with 26 Pictures. For the Ufe of Schools. Fifth Edition, with Additions. By James Greenwood, Author of the Englifh Grammar, and Sur-Mafter of St. Paul's School, price 1 s

Some

BOOKS *Printed for*

Some Improvements to the Art of Teaching especially in the first grounding a young Scholar in Grammar-Learning, shewing a short, sure and easy way to bring a Scholar to Variety and Elegancy in writing Latin : Written for the help and ease of all School-Masters and Ushers The 8th Edition very much corrected. By William Walker, B D Author of the Treatise of Idioms and Particles, &c. price 1 s

Phædri, Cæsaris Augusti Liberti, Fabularum Æsopiarum, Libri quinti ablii Syri Sententiæ ex ejus mimis col ○ ⊷ ..lto locupletiores Utrumque recensu t ⋇ notulas adjecit Sam Hoadley, A M scholæ Norvicensis quondam Magister, Editio quarta 1 s

Exercitia Latina, or, Latin for Garretson's English Exercises, for school Boys to translate Syntaxically By N Bayley, School Master The 4th Edition, Corrected and Improved. Price 1 s

More English Examples to be turn'd into Latin beginning with the Nominative Case and Verb as tis vary'd throughout all Moods and Tenses and after fitted to the Rules of Grammar To which are added some Cautions for Children to avoid Mistakes in making Latin, Forms of Epistles Themes, or other Exercises For the Use of Young Beginners at Bury School The 11th Edition, with large Additions, price 1 s.

Methodus Græcam Linguam docendi, (multa Grammaticorum arte omissa) ad Puerorum captum accommodata, & ab Edvardo Leedes (cui id Rei nuper creditum fuit intra Scholam Buriensem, in Pago Suffolciensi) in Usum Discipulorum tradita, & m in Usum Scholæ Gyppovecensis edita Editio tertia, plurimis Emendationibus, p s 6 d

Senten

A. Bettelworth, *and* J. Battley.

Sententiæ Græcæ, è variis Græcorum libris hinc inde excerptæ Quibus adduntur aurea Carmina Pythagoræ , & Epitaphium Adonidis, Bione Smirnæo Authore. Quæ omnia e Græco in Latinum Sermonem de verbo fere funt reddita, Subjungitur denique Tabula, non folum ad quam Orationis partem, fed & ad quod in Grammatica. Græca Exemplum in unumquodque Vocabulum (feu Nomen, feu Verbum, feu Participium, fic formandum eft, indicans In ufum Imprimis eorum qui Grecarum Literarum funt rudis. F. R. A M Editio Secunda. Price 1 s 6 d.

Familiaria Collcquia. Opera Chriftophori Helvici D & Profefforis Gieffenfis olim, & Erafmo Roterodamo Ludovico Vive, & Schollenio Haffo Sileɛta Editio Decima. Price 1s.

Cole's Latin Dictionary.
Horatius
Ovidii Metamorphofis
Martialis Epigrammata
Salluftius
L Florus
Terentius
Juvenal
Juftinus
} Cum Notis in Ufum Sereniffimi Delphini.
Xenophon de lyri Inftitutione.
Homeri Ilias.
Pantheon.

FINIS.

THE
PREFACE.

HERE *submit to the Judgment of the* Publick, *this* new Method *of Assisting* Young Beginners *in the* Exercises *of rendring* English *into* Latin, *and if those who are concern'd in* Teaching, *shall in the main approve the* Help *offered,* I *hope they will overlook with* Candour, *such Errors as may have arisen either from* Myself *or the* Press, *as* I *have used my utmost* Endeavours *to avoid* both.

The PREFACE.

both. It *is intended as an* Essay *for the more easy and* expeditious Initiation *of* Tyroes, *and therefore* Plainness *and* Perspicuity *is the principal* View *and* Aim *thro' the whole; and if upon* Trial *it shall be* judg'd *in some* Measure *to have answered the* End *designed, in being useful to* Master *and* Scholar, *I shall think myself sufficiently recompenced in that* Advantage, *nor regard the little* Cavils *that may be raised against it by those who* delight *in* Censure.

To

TO
Francis Child, Efq;

Alderman of the CITY of
LONDON,

AND

Prefident of CHRIST-
HOSPITAL.

SIR,

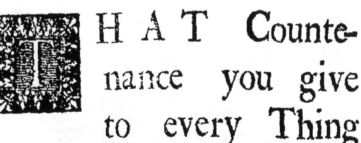

THAT Counte-
nance you give
to every Thing
intended for the *Service*
of this *HOSPITAL,*

A 2   and

and that Affability, with which You Receive every One concern'd in, and defirous to promote, that Good WORK, will, I hope, excufe this my Prefumption in Infcribing to You this new *Praxis* intended for the Benefit and Advantage of thofe Children, the Care of whofe Education is committed unto Me ; but more efpecially fo, as it

The Dedication.

is the first Opportunity
of publishing to the World
that grateful Sense I have
of your kind Inclinations
to me, and of that high
Esteem, and great Venera-
tion which You will always
command from,

SIR,

Your most Obedient,
Humble Servant,

PETER SELBY.

SENTENCES

Selected out of SOLOMON's PROVERBS, and ECCLESIASTES, for the Use of SCHOOLS.

Adversity.

IF thou faint in the day of *Adversity*, thy strength is small, *Chap* 24. 10.

2. A Friend loveth at all times, and a Brother is born for *Adversity*, 17 17.

3. In the day of Prosperity be joyful, but in the day of *Adversity* consider, *Eccles.* 7. 14.

Adultery.

1 By means of an whorish Woman, a Man is brought to a piece of bread, and the *Adulteress* will hunt for the precious life, 6 26.

2 Such is the way of an *adulterous* Woman, she eateth, and wipeth her mouth, and saith, I have done no wickedness. 32 20.

3 Whoso committeth *Adultery* with a Woman, lacketh understanding: He that doth it, destroys his own Soul, 6 32

Affliction.

1. All the days of the *afflicted* are evil; but he that is of a merry heart, hath a continual Feast. 15 15.

Anger.

E Proverbiis SOLOMONIS
Et Ecclesiaste Extracta
In usum SCHOLARUM.

Adversity.

1. SI tu [1] deficio in tempus [2] angustia, [3] tuus virtus [1] sum [17] angustus. *Cap* 24. *ver* 10

2 Amicus [1] diligo [2] omnis [4] tempus, & frater [1] nascor in angustia 17 17

3 In tempus [2] bonum [5] lætor, autem in tempus [2] malum [5] considero *Eccles* 7 14

Adultery.

1 Quisquis [1] perpetro [6] adulterium cum mulier, [7] careo [8] intelligentia [3] qui [9] facio [6+2] iste, [7] perdo [6] animus [3] suus *Prov* 6 32

2 [14] Is [1] sum via [3] scortans [2] mulier, [7] comedo & [10] abstergo [3] suus [6] os, & [10] dico, [7] operor [3] nullus [6] iniquitas. 30. 20

3. Propter [3] scortans mulier homo [1] deduco ad frustum [2] panis, & adultera [1] venor [2] pretiosus [6] vita 6 26

Affliction.

1. [3] Omnis dies [2] afflictus [1] sum [17] malus; sed [11] qui [1] sum [3] lætus animus, [7] habeo [2] continuus [6] convivium. 15 15

Anger.

1 The discretion of a man deferreth his *Anger*, and it is his glory to pass over a transgression 19 11

2 He that is flow to *Anger*, is better than the mighty, and he that ruleth his spirit, than he that taketh a city 16 32

3 Make no friendship with an *angry* man, and with a furious man thou shalt not go, left thou learn his ways, and get a snare to thy foul 22 24, 25

4 An *angry* man ftirreth up ftrife, and a furious man aboundeth in transgression 29 22

5 He that is foon *angry*, dealeth foolishly, and a man of wicked devices is hated. 14. 17

6 Be not hafty in fpirit to be *angry*, for *Anger* refteth in the bofom of fools Eccl f 7 9

Answer.

1 A man hath joy by the *Answer* of his mouth, and a word fpoke in due feafon, how good is it? 15 23

2 The heart of the righteous ftudieth to *Answer*, but the mouth of the wicked poureth out evil things 15 28

3 Every man shall kifs his lips that giveth a right *Answer* 24 26

4 A foft *Answer* turneth away wrath, but grievous words ftir up anger 15 1

5 *Answer* not a fool according to his folly, left thou alfo be like unto him 26 4

6 *Answer* a fool according to his folly, left he be wife in his own conceit. 26 5

7 He that *answereth* a matter before he heareth it, it is folly and shame unto him. 18. 13

8 The preparations of the heart in man, and the *Answer* of the tongue, is from the Lord 16 1.

Babbler.

Anger

1 Intellectus - homo ˈ defero ˑ ſuus ⁶ ira, &
ˑ ſum ˀ is ˈ ornamentum prætereo ⁰ defectio.
19 11

2 Qui ⁰ ſum ¹⁴ tardus ad ira ˉ ſum ¹⁴ melior
¹⁵ robuſtus, & qui ⁹ moderor ² ſuus ¹⁶ ſpiritus ¹¹ is
ˉ qui ⁹ capio ⁶ civitas 16 32

3 ⁵ Exerceo ˀ nullus ⁵ amicitia cum iracundus & cum furibundus non ⁵ congredior, ne ⁵ diſ-
co ⁵ iter -is & ¹³ aſſuno ⁵ tendicula ˀ tuus ˈ anima. 22 24, 25.

4 Iracundus ˈ excito ⁶ contentio, & furibundus ˈ abundo ⁸ defectio 29 22

5 Qui ⁹ ſum ciro ¹⁴ iratus ˉ facio ſtulte, &
homo ¹⁵ cogitatio ˀ fraudulentus ¹⁹ odium ˈ habeor. 14 17

6 Ne ⁵ perturbo in ſpiritus ut ˀ indignor, nam
indignatio ˈ conquieſco in ſinus - ſtultus E. 7 9

Anſwer.

1 Homo ˈ habeo ⁶ lætitia ex ſermo ³ ſuus ² es,
& verbum ³ prolatus ˀ debitus ·⁹ tempus quam
ˀ bonus ˈ ſum. 15 23

2 Animus ² juſtus ˈ meditor ad ²⁰ reſpondeo,
autem os ² improbus ˈ eructo ⁶ malus. 15. 28.

3 Unus quiſque ˈ oſculor ⁶ labium ² is, ˉqui
ˀ reddo ˑ rectus ⁶ reſponſum 24 26

4 ³ Mollis reſponſio ˈ averto ⁶ excandeſcentia,
autem verbum ˀ moleſtus ˈ excito ⁶ ira. 15 ⅰ

5 Ne ⁵ reſpondeo ²¹ ſtolidus ſecundum ſtultitia
² is, ne tu quoque ˈ ſum ¹⁴ ſimilis ²² ille. 26 4

6 ⁵ Reſpondeo ²¹ ſtolidus ſecundum ſtultitia
² is, ne ˀ ſum ¹⁴ ſapiens in oculus ³ ſuus 26 5.

7 Qui ⁹ reſpondeo ²¹ aliquis priuſquam ˀ audio,
¹² ſum ¹⁵ ſtultitia & ²³ ignominia ²¹ is 18 13

8 Præparatio ² cor in homo & ²⁰ reſponſio
- lingua ⁵⁰ ſum a Dominus 16. 1.

Babbler

Babbler.

1 The Serpent will bite without enchantment, and a *Babbler* is no better *Ecccf* 10 11

Backslider.

1 The *Backslider* in heart shall be filled with his own ways, and a good man shall be satisfied from himself 14 14

Blessing.

1 The *Blessing* of the Lord it maketh rich, and he addeth no sorrow with it 10 22

2 *Blessings* are upon the head of the just, but violence covereth the mouth of the wicked 10 6

Blood thirsty

1 The *Blood thirsty* hate the upright, but the Just seek his soul 29 10

Brother.

1. A *Brother* offended is harder to be won than a strong City, and their contentions are like the bars of a Castle 18 19

2 Thine own friend and thy Father's friend forsake not, neither go into thy *Brother's* house in the day of thy calamity for better is a neighbour that is near, than a *Brother* that is far off. 27 10

Cause.

1 He that is first in his own *Cause* seemeth just, but his neighbour cometh and searcheth him. 18 17

2 Debate thy *Cause* with thy neighbour himself, and discover not a secret to another. 25 9

3 Open thy mouth for the dumb in the *Cause* of all such as are appointed to destruction. 31 8.

Chasten

Babbler.

1. Serpens ¹mordeo fine incantatio, & garru-lus no¹ ¹fum ¹⁷ melior *Ecclef.* 10 11

Backflider.

1. Tergiverfator in animus ¹fatio ²fuus 8 via, & vir ² bonus, ¹fatio à fui ³ ipfe 14 14.

Bleffing.

1. Benedictio ² Jehova ² ipfe ¹dito, & ⁷ ad-do ³ nullus ⁶ moleftia cum ³ is 10 22

2. Benedictio ¹ adfum ¹⁷caput ²juftus, at violentia ¹ ol tego ⁶ os ² impius. 10 6

Blood-thirfty.

1. Sanguinarius ¹ odi ⁶ integer, autem rectus ¹ quæro ⁶ anima ² i. 29 10

Brother.

1. Frater ³ provocatus ¹ fum ¹⁴ difficilior ⁻⁴ vinco ¹⁵ urbs ³ munitus, & contentio ²x³ hic ¹ fum ut ²³ vectis ² arx 18 19

2. ³ Tuus ⁶amicus & ² paternus ²⁹ amicus ne ⁵ derelinquo, nec ⁵ ingredior ⁶ domus ² tuus frater ¹⁹ tempus ³ tuus ² calamitas, nam ¹⁴ melior ¹ fum vicinus ³ propinquus ¹⁵ frater longinquus 27 10

Caufe.

1. Qui ⁵ fum ¹⁴ primus in lis ³ fuus ⁷ videor ¹⁴ juftus, autem proximus ² is ¹ advenio & ¹⁰ inveftigo ⁶+² is. 17 18

2. ⁵ Ago ⁶ caufa ² tuus cum proximus ³ tuus ipfe, fed ne ⁵ retego ⁶ arcanum ²¹ alter 25 9

3. ⁵ Aperio ⁶ os ² tuus pro mutus in caufa ² omnis ⁻+² ille ³ qui ⁹ trado ²⁵ excidium ³ 8.

Chasten.

1 My Son despise not the Chastening of the Lord, re ther be weary of his correction 3 11

2 Chasten thy Son whilst there is hope, and let not thy soul spare for his crying. 19 18

3 He that spareth his Rod, hateth his Son, but he that loveth him, chasteneth him betimes 13 24

Child

1 Even a Child is known by his doings, whether his work be pure, and whether it be right 20 11.

2 Foolishness is bound in the heart of a Child, but the rod of correction shall drive it far from him 22 15.

3 With-hold not correction from the Child, for if thou beatest him with a Rod, he shall not die 23 13

4. The rod and reproof give wisdom, but a Child left to himself bringeth his Mother to shame 29 15

5 The Father of the righteous shall greatly rejoice, and he that begetteth a wise Child shall have joy of him. 23 24.

6 Better is a poor and wife Child, than an old and foolish king, who will no more be admonished Ecclef 4 13

7 There is one alone, and there is not a second; yea, he hath neither Child nor Brother yet is there no end of all his labour neither is his eye satisfied with riches, neither faith he, for whom do I labour and bereave my soul of good? Ecclef 4 8.

8 Children. Children are the crown of old men, and the glory of Children are their Fathers 17 6.

Chaſſeu.

1 · Méus 2 filius ne 5 ſperno 6 erudit o - Je-hova, neque 2 tædet 28 tu 28 correctio 2 is 3 11.

2 5 Caſtigo 6 filius 2 tuus dum 1 ſum ſpes, nec animus 3 tuus 1 condono propter clamor 2 ipſe 19 18

3 Qui 9 cohibeo 6 virga 2 ſuus, 7 odi 6 filius 2 ſuus, autem qui 9 amo 2 is, 7 caſtigo 6 + 2 ille tempeſtivè 13 24.

Chud.

1 Etiam per 1 cognoſco 9 actio 2 ſuus, an o-pus 1 ſum 14 purus, & an 10 ſum 14 rectus 20 11.

2 Stultitia alligo 17 animus 2 puer, autem virga 2 eruditio 1 amoveo 2 s 6 x 3 procul ab 5 ipſe. 22 15

3 Ne 5 ſubtraho 6 correctio à puer, enim ſi percutio 6 x 2 is 2 virga, non 7 morior. 23 13.

4 Virga & 2 correptio 30 do 6 ſapientia, at puer permiſſus 2 ſui 1 pudefacio 6 mater 3 ſu-is. 29 15

5 Pater 2 juſtus valde 1 exulto, & qui 9 gig-no 2 ſapiens 6 puer 7 lætor de 3 is 23 4

6 14 Melior 1 ſum 3 indigus & 5 ſapiens puer ſenex & 2 ſtolidus 15 Rex, qui 9 vo o non am-plius 21 admoneo Ecleſ 4 1

7 1 Sum 2 unus 3 aliquis & 1 ſum non 2 ſe-cundus, imo 7 hileo nec 6 filius nec 2 frater, nec tamen 1 ſum finis 2 omnis 3 is 2 labor, nec 2 is oculus 1 ſatio 6 divitiæ, nec 7 dico 11 qui ego 1 laboro & 10 deſtituo 6 anima 2 meus 2 bo-num 2 Ecleſ 4 8

8 Filius 2 filius 1 ſum 2 corona 2 ſenex, & 2 ornamentum 2 filius 1 ſum 3 pater 2 ipſe 17 6.

9 If a man beget an hundred *Children*, and live many years, so that the days of his years be many, and his soul be not filled with good, and also that he have no burial, I say an untimely Birth is better than he *Ecclef* 6 9

10 Train up a *Child* in the way he should go, and when he is old, he will not depart from it 22 6

11 I considered all the living which walk under the Sun, with the second *Child* that shall stand up in his stead *Ecclef* 4 15

City
1 The labour of the foolish wearieth every one of them because he knoweth not how to go to the City *Ecclef* 10 15

Cord.
1 If one prevail against him two shall withstand him and a three fold *Cord* is not quickly broken *Ecclef* 4 12

Crooked.
1 That which is *crooked* cannot be made strait, and that which is wanting cannot be number'd. *Ecclef* 1 15

Confidence.
1 Confidence in an unfaithful man in time of trouble, is like a broken tooth, and a foot out of joint 25 9

2 A wise man feareth and departeth from evil, but the fool rageth and is *confident* 14 16

Commandment.
1 Whoso despiseth the word, shall be destroyed, but he that feareth the *Commandment*, shall be rewarded 13 13

2 He that keepeth the *Commandment*, keepeth his own soul, but he that despiseth his ways, shall die 19 16

3 The

9 Si vir ¹ gigno ⁶ liberi ³ centenus, &
¹⁰ vivo ³ multus ³² annus adeo ut dies ² annus
² is ¹ fum ¹⁴ multus & anima ² is non ¹ fatio
⁸ bonum, & nec ¹ fum fepultura 45 is, ⁵ dico
⁵⁵ abortivus ²⁴ fum ⁵⁶ melior ¹⁵ ille *Ecchf* 6 3.

10. ⁵ Inftruo ⁶ puer in via, qui ¹⁹ + ³ qui oportet 33 is ²⁴ eo, & cum ⁷ fenefco, non ⁷ recedo ab
˜ is 22 6

11 ⁵ Video ³ omnis ⁶ vivus ³ qui ⁹ ambulo fub
fol cum ⁵ fecundus puer, ³ qui ⁹ fto ¹⁹ locus
˜ 1ᶜ. *Ecclef* 4 15.

City.

1 Labor ² ftolidus ¹ fatigo ⁶ quifque ⁵⁴ ipfe,
quoniam ⁷ nefcio ²⁴ eo in civitas *Eccl-f* 10, 15.

Cord.

1 Si unus ¹ vinco ⁶ + ³ is, duo ¹ obfifto
˜ ille, & ³ triplicatus filum non cito ¹ abrum-
po. *Ecclef* 4 12

Crooked.

1 Qui ⁹ fum ¹⁴ perverfus non ¹² poffum
²⁷ corrigo, & qui ⁹ deficio non ¹⁴ poffum ²⁴ numero *Ecclf* 1 15

Confidence.

1 Fiducia in perfidus ¹⁹ dies ² anguftia, ¹ fum
ut ˜ fractus ²³ dens & ²⁵ pes ³ luxatus 25 19.

2 Sapiens ¹ timeo & ¹⁰ recedo a malum, ve-
rò ftolidus ¹ excandefco & ¹⁰ fum ¹⁴ fecurus.
14 16

Commandment.

1 Quifquis ¹ contemno ⁶ verbum ⁷ corrumpor, autem qui ⁹ revereor ⁶ præceptum, ⁷ rependor 13 13

2 Qui ⁹ obfervo ⁶ præceptum, ⁷ fervo ⁶ anima ³ fuus, autem qui ⁹ fperno ³ fuus ⁶ via,
⁷ morior. 19 16.

B 5 3. Sapiens

2 The wise in heart will receive Commandment, but a prating fool shall fall 10 8

Comely.

1 There be three things that go well, yea four are comely in going, a Lion, which is the strongest among beasts, and turneth not away from any, a Grey-hound, and an He goat also, and a King, against whom there is no rising up 30 29, 30, 31

Contentious.

1 As coals are to burning coals and wood to fire, so is a contentious man to kindle strife 26 21

Corn.

1 He that with-holdeth Corn, the people shall curse him, but blessing shall be upon the head of him that selleth it 11 26

Correct.

1 Correct thy son, and he shall give thee rest yea he shall give delight unto thy soul 29 17

2 Correction is grievous unto him that forsaketh the way, and he that hateth reproof shall die 5 10

3 A servant will not be corrected by words, for though he understand he will not answer 29 19

Counsel.

1 Where no counsel is, the people fall, but in the multitude of Counsellors there is safety 11 14

2 Hear Counsel, and receive instruction, that thou mayest be wise in thy latter end. 19 20

3 Without Counsel purposes are disappointed, but in the multitude of Counsellors they are established 15 22

4 Every purpose is established by Counsel, and with good advice make war 20 18

5 Counsel

3 Sapiens 7 animus 1 accipio 6 præceptum,
sed 3 loquax stultus 1 cado 10 8

Comely.

1 1 Sum tres qui 9 procedo, imo quatuor
1 sum 14 decorus in 5 ambulo, Leo 2 qui 9 sum
robustissimus inter bestia, nec 10 retrogredior
metus 2 quisquam, vertagus, & 2 caper etiam, & 2 rex in qui 1 sum nullus insurrectio.
30 29, 30 31.

Contentious.

1 Ut carbo 1 sum ad pruna, & lignum ad
ignis, ita 1 sum 3 contentiosus vir ad accendo lis 26 21

Corn.

1 Qui 9 retineo 6 triticum, populus 1 execror ei 1 ille aurem benedictio 1 incumbo
caput vendens ille 11 26

Correct.

1 5 Castigo tuus 6 filius & offero te
6 quies imo do delicia tuus 6 anima 29 17.
1 Correptio 1 sum gravis ei 5
iter, & qui 5 odi correptio mo

Servus non 1 castigo te
vis intelligo, non respondeo 29 19

Counsel.

1 Ubi nullus consilium 1 sum, populus
corruo, autem in multitudo consiliarius
salus 11 14
2 1 Ausculto consilium, & 10 accipio 6 eruditio ut 5 sapio in dies tuus ultimus 19 20
3 Sine consilium cogitatio 1 fio 14 irritus
at in multitudo 2 consiliarius 1 stabilior 15 22

4 1 Unusquisque propositum 1 confirmor consilium & prudens consilium 1 gero 6 bellum. 20. 18.

5 Counsel in the heart of man is like deep waters, but a man of understanding will draw it out 20 5

6 There are many devices in a man's heart; nevertheless the *counsel* of the Lord that shall stand. 19 21

7 Ointment and perfume rejoyce the heart; so doth the sweetness of a man s friend by hearty *counsel* 27 9

8 The thoughts of the righteous are right; but the *counsels* of the wicked are deceit 12 5

9 Deceit is in the heart of them that imagine evil but to the *counsellors* of peace is joy. 12 20.

Cobrr.

1 He that covers to a transgression, seeketh love but he that repeateth a matter, separateth very friends. 17 9

2 He that *covereth* his sins shall not prosper: but whoso confesseth and forsaketh them, shall have mercy 28 13

Curse.

1 The *curse* of the Lord is in the house of the wicked but he blesseth the habitation of the just 3 33

2 As the Bird by wandring, as the Swallow by flying, so the *curse* causeless shall not come. 26 2

3 He that giveth unto the poor shall not lack, but he that hideth his eyes, shall have many a *curse*. 28 27

Deceit.

1. Bread of *deceit* is sweet to a man, but afterwards his mouth shall be fill d with gravel. 20, 17

2 He that hateth, dissembleth with his lips, and layeth up the *deceit* within him 26 24.

3 Whose

5 Confilium in animus [2] vir [1] fum [14] fimilis [2] profundus [22] aqua, tamen vir [3] intelligens
[1] haurio [6] + [2] ille 20. 5

6 [1] Infum [3] multus cogitatio [17] animus [2] homo, fed confilium [2] Jehova [3] ipfe [1] fto 19. 21

7 Unguentum & [22] fuffitus [30] lætifico [6] cor ;
it [1] dulcedo - amicus [3] fuus [2] cordatus [29] confilium 27 9,

8 Cogitatio [2] juftus [1] fum [14] juftus & confilium [2] improbus [1] fum [13] dolus. 12 5

9 Dolus [1] fum in cor [2] fabricans [21] malum ;
autem [21] confiliarius [2] pax [1] fum lætitia. 12 20.

Cober.

1. Qui [9] tego [6] defectio, [7] quæro [6] dilectio ;
vero qui [9] renovo [6] res [7] disjungo etiam [6] a-
micus 17 9

2 Qui [9] tego [3] fuus [6] defectio non [7] fuccedo ;
vero qui [9] fateor & [10] derelinquo [6] + [3] is, [7] invenio [6] mifericordia. 28. 13.

Curfe.

1 Execratio [2] Jehova [1] incumbo [17] domus
[2] improbus , at [7] benedico [17] habitaculum [2] juftus. 3 33

2 Ut avicula [29] erro, ut hirundo [38] volito, ita
maledictio [3] immeritus non [1] advenio. 26 2.

3 Qui [9] do [25] pauper non [7] egeo, vero [11] is
qui [9] occulto [6] oculus [3] fuus, [1] fum [3] multus
maledictio. 28 27.

Deceit.

1 Cibus [2] falfitas [1] fum [14] fuavis [22] vir, fed
poftea os [2] is [1] impleo [8] fcrupus 20 17.

2 Qui [9] odi, [1] fimulo [3] fuus [29] labium, &
[10] repono [6] dolus intra fui. 26. 24.

3. Qui

3 Whose hatred is covered by deceit, his wickedness shall be shewed before the whole congregation 26 26

4 Faithful are the wounds of a friend, but the kisses of an enemy are deceitful 27 6

5 The poor and the deceitful man meet together, the Lord lightneth both their eyes 29 13

Desire

1 The desire accomplished is sweet to the soul, but it is is abomination to fools to depart from evil 13 19

2 The desire of a man is his kindness, and a poor man is better than a liar 19 22

Despised.

1 A man shall be commended according to his wisdom, but he that is of a perverse heart shall be despised 12 8

He that is despised, and hath a servant, is better than he that is honoured and lacketh bread 12 9

Destruction

1 Before destruction the heart of man is haughty, and before honour is humility 18 12

2 Pride goeth before destruction, and a haughty spirit before a fall 16 18

3 Hell and destruction are never full, so the eyes of a man are never satisfied 27 20

Diligent.

1 The hand of the diligent shall bear rule, but the slothful hand shall be under tribute 12 24

2 He becometh poor that dealeth with a slack hand, but the hand of the diligent maketh rich 10 4

3 The slothful man roasteth not that which he took in hunting, but the substance of a diligent man is precious. 12 27

3 ⁷Qui odium ¹tegor ²⁹deceptio, malitia
is ¹revelo coram ⁷totus congregatio .6 26

4 ¹⁴Fidelis ¹ſum vulnus ²amicus, verum
oſculum ²inimicus ¹ſum ¹⁴doloſus 27 6

5 Pauper & doloſus homo ⁷occurro una,
Jehova ¹illumino ⁶oculus -+⁷ ambo. 29 13.

Deſiſc.

1 Deſiderium ⁷effectus ¹ ſum ¹⁴ ſuavis ²⁻ a-
nima, at ¹² ſum ¹ abominatio ² ſtolidus recedo
a malum 13. 19

2 Deſiderium ²homo ¹ſum ²is ⁷ benignita-
tis, & pauper ¹¹ſum ¹⁴ melior ¹⁵ mendax 19 ⁻2

Deſpiſco.

1 Vir ¹ laudor ſecundum intellectus , ſed
¹ qui ⁷ ſum ⁵ perverſus animus ⁷⁻contemnor.
12 8

2 Qui ⁹contemnor & ¹⁰habeo ⁶ſervus, ⁻ſum
¹ melior ¹⁵ x ⁻ is qui ⁹extollo ⁶ ſui & ¹⁰ egeo
⁹cibus. 12 9

Deſtruction.

1 Ante perditio animus ²homo ¹extollo
⁶ ſui, & ante honor ¹ ſum abjectio ₁8 12

2 Superbia ¹eo ante perditio, & ⁻³ ſpiritus
elatus ante lapſus. 16 18

3 Sepulcrum & ²³ perditio nunquam ³⁰ ſatio ,
ita oculus ² homo nunquam ¹ ſatio 27 20

Diligent.

1 Manus ² ſedulus ¹ dominor, autem manus
ignavus ¹ ſum ¹⁴ tributarius 12 24

2 ⁷ Fio ¹⁴ pauper qui ⁹ ago ³ ignavus ²⁷ manus, autem manus ² ſedulus ¹ dito 10 4

3 Ignavus ¹ aſſo non ⁶ is ⁹+³ qui ⁷ capio ²⁷ venor, autem ſubſtantia ² ſedulus ¹ ſum ¹⁴ pretioſus. 12. 27

4 Anima

4 The foul of the fluggard defireth and hath nothing, but the foul of the *Diligent* shall be made fat. 13 3

5 The thoughts of the *diligent* tend only to plenteoufnefs but of every one that is hafty, only to want. 21. 5

6 Seeft thou a man *diligent* in his bufinefs? he shall stand before Kings, he shall not stand before mean men 22 29

7 He that *diligently* seeketh good, procureth favour but he that seeketh mischief, it shall come unto him 11 27

Dreams.

1 In the multitude of *Dreams* and many words there are alfo divers vanities but fear thou God *Ecclef* 5 7.

2 A *dream* cometh through multitude of bufinefs, and a fool's voice is known by a multitude of words *Ecclef* 5 3

Ear.

1 The heart of the prudent getteth knowledge, and the *ear* of the wife feeketh knowledge 18 15

2 The hearing *ear*, and the feeing *eye*, the Lord hath made even both of them, 20 12.

3 He that turneth away his *ear* from hearing the Law, even his prayer shall be abomination. 28. 29

Eat.

1 *Eat* thou not the bread of him that hath an evil eye, neither defire thou his dainty meats.23 6

Earth.

1 The profit of the *earth* is for all, the King himfelf is ferved by the field *Ecclef* 5 9

Enemy.

1 Rejoyce not when thine *enemy* falleth; and let not thine heart be glad when he ftumbleth. 24. 17.

2 If

4 Anima ²piger ¹defidero & ¹⁰habeo ⁵ni-
hil, vero anima ²fedulus ¹efficio ¹⁴pinguis.
13 3

5 Cogitatio ²fedulus ¹tendo tantum ad co-
pa . autem ²omnis ²præceps, tantum ad egeftas 21 5

6 ⁵Viderne ⁶vir ³diligens in ⁵fuus opus ?
confifto ante Rex, non ⁷confifto ante obfcu-
rus. 22 29

7 Qui ftudiofe ⁶quæro ⁶bonum, ⁷conqui-
10 ⁶benevolentia · vero qui ⁹quæro ⁶malum,
evenio -¹ipfe 11 27

Dreams

1 In multitudo ²Somnium & ³multus - verbum ¹infum etiam ³varius vanitas fed ¹re-
vereor tu ⁶Deus *Ecclef* 5. 7

2 Somnium ¹prodo ²⁹multitudo ²occupa-
tio, & vox ²ftolidus ¹cognofcor ²⁹multitudo
²verbum. *Ecclef* 5 3

Ear.

1. Animus ²prudens ¹poffideo ⁶fcientia, &
auris ²fapiens ¹quæro ⁶fcientia 18 15

2. ⁵Audiens ⁶auris, & ³videns ²³oculus,
Jehova ¹facio æque ³⁰uterque ³⁴+³is. 20 12

3 Qui ⁹averto ³fuus ⁶auris ab ³⁸audio
lex, etiam oratio ²is ¹fum ¹³abominatio.
28 9

Eat.

1. ¹Edo tu ne ⁶cibus ²is ¹¹qui ¹fum ³malig-
nus oculus, nec ⁵defidero ⁶cupeliæ ²ille. 23 6

Earth.

1. Emolumentum ²terra ¹fum pro omnis,
Rex ³ipfe ¹fuppeditor ex ager *Ecclef* 5 9

Enemy.

1 ⁵Lætor ne quum ³tuus inimicus ¹cado,
neque animus ³tuus ¹exulto quum ⁷titubo.
24 17.

1 If thine enemy be hungry, give him bread to eat, and if he be thirsty, give him water to drink 25 21

Envy.

1 Envy thou not the oppressor, and choose none of his ways 3 31

2 Let not thine heart envy sinners, but be thou in the fear of the Lord all the day long 23 17

3 A sound heart is the life of the flesh, but envy is the rottenness of the bones. 14 30

4 Wrath is cruel and anger is outragerous, but who is able to stand before envy? 27 4

Evil

1 The evil bow before the good, and the wicked at the gates of the righteous 14 19

2 Evil men understand not judgment, but they that seek the Lord understand all things 28 5

3 In the transgression of an Evil man there is a snare, but the righteous do sing and rejoyce 29 6

4 Do they not err that devise Evil? but mercy and truth shall be to them that devise good 14 22

5 Whoso rewardeth Evil for Good, Evil shall not depart from his house 17 13

Eye.

1 He that winketh with the Eye causeth sorrow, but a prating fool shall fall 10 10

2 He that hath a bountiful Eye shall be blessed, for he giveth of his bread to the poor 22 9

3 The Eye that mocketh at his Father, and despiseth to obey his Mother, the Ravens of the Valley shall pick it out, and the young Eagles shall eat it 30 17.

1 Si tuus inimicus [1] efurio [5] do [25] ille [6] panis ut [7] edo, & fi [7] fitio [5] do [25] is [6] aq a ut [1] b bo. 25 21

Enby.

1 [1] Invideo tu ne [21] violentus, & [10] eligo [1] nullus [6] via [2] is 3 31

2 Ne animus [3] tuus [1] æmulor [21] peccator, fed [5] fum in reverentia [2] Jehova [2] totus [4] dies 23 17

3 [1] Sanus animus [1] fum [13] vita [2] caro, vero invidia [1] fum [13] putredo [1] os 14 30

4 Excandefcentia [1] fum [11] crudelis, & ira [1] fum [14] infanus, fed quis [1] poffum [24] confifto coram invidia ? 27 4

Evil.

1 Malus [1] incurvo coram bonus, & [1] improbus ad porta [2] juftus 14 19.

2 [3] Malus homo [1] animadverto non [6] jus, autem [3] quærens [31] Jehova [1] animadverto [6] omnis 28 5

3 [1] Defectio [2] vir malus [1] infum tendicula, autem juftus [1] canto & [10] lætor. 29 6

4 [7] Erro nonne qui [9] meditor [6] malum ? vero mifericordia & [2] fides [30] fum [21] meditans [31] bonum 14 22

5 Quifquis [1] reddo [6] malum pro bonum, malum non [1] recedo a domus [2] ille. 17 13

Eye.

1. Qui [9] nicto [29] oculus [7] do [6] moleftia, at loquax ftultus [1] cado 10 10

2 Qui [9] habeo [3] benignus [6] oculus [7] benedico, nam [7] do de panis [5] fuus [25] indigus, 22 9

3 [6] Oculus qui [9] illudo [3] fuus [17] pater, & [1] fperno [24] obedio [3] fuus [41] mater, corvus [2] vallis [1] effodio [6] hic, & [1] juvenis aquila [1] comedo [6] is. 30 17.

4 All things are full of labour, man cannot utter it. The *Eye* is not satisfied with seeing, nor the ear filled with hearing *Eccl.f* 1 8.

5 The light of the *Eyes* rejoiceth the heart, and a good report maketh the bones fat. 15 30.

6 The *Eyes* of the Lord are in every place beholding the evil and the good. 15 3

7 The *Eyes* of the Lord preserve knowledge and he overthroweth the words of the transgressors 22 12

8 The wise man's *Eyes* are in his head, but the fool walketh in darknefs *Eccl f* 2 14

9 Better is the sight of the *Eyes* than the wandring of the desire *Eccles* 6 9

10 Be not wife in thine own *Eyes*, fear the Lord and depart from ev l 3 7

11 The way of a fool is right in his own eyes, but he that hearkeneth unto counfel is wife 12. 15.

12 Every way of a man is right in his own E s, but the Lord pondereth the hearts. 21. 2.

13 There is a generation that are pure in their own *Eyes*, and yet is not wafhed from their own filthinefs

14 Let thine *Eyes* look right on, and let thine eye-lids look ftrait before thee 4 25

Face.

1 A man's wifdom maketh his *Face* to fhine, and the boldnefs of his *Face* fhall be changed Ec f 8 1

Father.

1 Hearken unto thy *Father* that begat thee, and defpife not thy Mother when fhe is old. 23. 22

2 Hear ye children the inftruction of a *Father*, and attend to know underftanding 4 1

4 ⸱ Singulus res ꞌ ſum ꞌ⁴ plenus ⁴ᶜ l. bor, vir
ꞌnon poſſum ²⁴ eloquoꞌ , oculus non ꞌ ſatior ꝫ⁸ vi-
den, nec auꞌis ꞌ impleor ꞌ⁰ audio *Ecclef* ꞌ 8

5 Lumen ꞌ⁄ oculus ꞌ læꞌifico ⁶ animus, &
bꞌnus fama ꞌ pinguefacio ⁶ os ꞌ5 ꝫ0

6 Oculus ꞌ⁄ Jehoꞌa ꞌ ſum in ꝫ omnis locus,
ſpeculans ꞌꞌ malus & ꞌ⁄ bonus ꞌ5 ꝫ

7 Oculus ꞌ⁄ Jehova ꞌ cuſtodio ⁶ ſcientia, au-
drm ⁷ perverto ⁶ verbum ꞌ⁄ perfidicſus. ꞌꞌ ꞌꞌ

8 ⸱ Sapiens oculus ꞌ ſum in ⸱ ſuus caput, au-
t m ſtolidus ꞌ ambuloin tenebræ *Ecclef* ꞌ ꞌ4

9 ꞌ⁴ Melior ꞌ ſum inſpectio ꞌ⁄ oculus quam
⸱ cuiſus ꞌ⁄ deſiderium *Ecclef* 6 9

ꞌ0 Ne ꞌ ſum ꞌ⁴ ſapiens ꞌ9 judicium ⸱ tuus.
⸱ꞌ revertor ⁶ Jehoꞌa & ꞌ0 recedo a malum ꝫ ⁷

ꞌꞌ Viꞌ ꞌ⁄ ſtultus ꞌ ſum ꞌ⁴ rectus in ꝫ ſuus
⸱ ccuꞌus, at ꞌꞌ qui 9 auſculto ⁴ꞌ conſilium ⁷ ſum
ꞌ⁴ ſapiens ꞌꞌ ꞌ5

ꞌꞌ ⸱ Unuſquiſqꞌꞌ via ꞌ⁄ homo ꞌ ſum ꞌ⁴ rectus
in ⸱ ſuus oculus, ſed Jehova ꞌ perpendo ⁶ animus ꞌꞌ ꞌ⁄

ꞌꝫ ꞌ Sum generaꞌio ꞌ⁴ mundus in ꝫ ſuus ccu-
lus, attamen non ꞌ abluor à ⸱ ſuus ſordes

ꞌ⁴ ⸱ Tuus occulus ꞌ intueor ex adverſus, &
tuus palpebra ꞌ ſpecto recta coram tu 4 ꞌ5.

· 𝕱𝖆𝖈𝖊.

ꞌ ꞌ⁄ Homo ſapientia ꞌ illuſtro ⁶ facies ꞌ⁄ ꞌs, &
firmitas ꞌ⁄ vultus ⸱ ille ꞌ mutor *Ecclef* 8. ꞌ

𝕱𝖆𝖙𝖍𝖊𝖗.

ꞌ Auſculto tuus ꞌꞌ pater ꝫ qui 9 gigno ⁵ tu,
neque ⁵ contemno ⸱ tuus ⁶ mater quum ⁷ ſeneſco.
ꞌꝫ ꞌꞌ

ꞌ⁄ ꞌ Audio ꞌ⁴ filius ⁶ eruditio ꞌ⁄ pater & ꞌ0 attendo ad ꞌ0 cognoſco ⸱9 prudentia. 4 ꞌ

                   ꝫ· Sapiens

3 A wise son maketh a glad *Father*, but a foolish son is the heaviness of his mother 10 1.

4 He that begetteth a fool, doth it to his sorrow and the *Father* of a fool hath no joy 17 21

5 A foolish son is a grief to his *Father*, and bitterness to her that bare him 17 25

6 He that wasteth his *Father*, and chaceth away his mother, is a son that causeth shame and bringeth reproach 19 26

7 A foolish son is the calamity of his *Father* and the contentions of a wife are a continual dropping 19 13

8 Whoso curseth his *Father* or his mother, his lamp shall be put out in obscure darkness 20 20

9 Whoso robbeth his *Father* or his mother, and saith it is no transgression, the same is the companion of a destroyer 28 24

Fear.

1 The *Fear* of the Lord prolongeth days, but the years of the wicked shall be shortned. 10 27

2 The *Fear* of the Lord is a fountain of Life, to depart from the snares of death 14 27

3 The *Fear* of the Lord is the instruction of wisdom, and before honour is humility 15. 33

4 The *Fear* of the Lord is to hate evil, pride and arrogancy, and the evil way, and the froward mouth do I hate. 8 13

5 In the *Fear* of the Lord is strong confidence and his Children shall have a place of refuge 14. 26

6 By mercy and truth iniquity is purged, and by the *fear* of the Lord men depart from evil 16 6

7 Better is little with the *fear* of the Lord, than great treasure and trouble therewith. 15 16

8. The

3 Sapiens filius ¹ facio ³ lætus ⁶ pater, vel ⁹ stolidus filius ¹ sum ¹⁵ mœstitia ²¹ mater ³ suus. 10 1

4 ⁹ Qui ⁹ gigno ⁶ stolidus ⁷ gigno ad mœror ⁹ suus, nec pater ⁻ stultus ¹ lætor. 17 21

5 ⁹ Stolidus filius ¹ sum ¹ dolor ⁹ suus ¹¹ pater & ⁺⁹ amaritudo ³ suus ²¹ genetrix 17 25

6 Qui ⁹ devasto ⁶ pater ⁹ suus & ¹⁰ fugo suus ⁶ mater, ⁷ sum ¹³ filius ³ qui ⁹ pudefacio intero ⁶ probrum 19 26

7 ⁹ Stolidus filius ⁻ sum ¹³ calamitas ⁹ suus pater, & jurgium ² mulier ¹ suum ⁹ continuus ⁻ illa 19 13

8 Qui ⁹ maledico suus ¹¹ pater aut ³ suus mater, lucerna ² is extinguo in ³ niger tenebræ 20 20.

9 Quisquis ¹ spolio ⁹ suus ⁶ pater aut ³ suus ⁻ mater, & ¹⁰ dico ²⁴ sum ³ nullus ⁶ defectio, idem ¹ sum ¹⁵ socius ² interfector 28 24

Fcat.

1 Reverentia ⁻ Jehova ¹ abjicio ⁶ dies, vero annus ² improbus ¹ decurro 10 27

2 Reverentia ⁻ Jehova ¹ sum ¹³ scaturigo ⁻ vita ad ²⁰ recedo a tendicula ² mors. 14. 27

3 Reverentia ² Jehova ¹ sum ¹⁵ eruditio ² sapientia, & ante honor ¹ sum abjectio. 15 33

4 Reverentia ² Jehova ¹⁰ sum odi ⁶ malum, ⁶ fastus & ²⁰ elatio & ²³ via ³ malus, & ²⁰ os perversus ⁵ odi, 8 13

5. In reverentia ² Jehova ¹ sum fiducia ³ validus, & ² is ¹¹ filius ¹ sum receptus 14 26

6 ⁻⁹ Benignitas & ²³ veritas iniquitas ¹ expior, & ²⁹ reverentia ² Jehova homo ¹ recedo à malum. 16 6

7 ¹⁴ Melior ¹ sum parvum cum reverentia Jehova, quam ³ amplus ²³ thesaurus & ²³ vexatio cum ³ ille. 15 16.　　　8. Reve-

F

8 The *fear* of the Lord tendeth to life, and he that hath it shall abide satisfied, he shall not be visited with evil 19 23

9 By humility and the *fear* of the Lord are riches, and honour, and life 22 4

10 *Fear* God and keep his commandments, for this is the whole duty of man *Ecclef* 12 13

11 Tho' a sinner do evil an hundred times, and his days be prolonged, yet surely I know that it shall be well with them that *fear* God, which *fear* before him *Ecclef* 8 12

12 My Son *fear* thou the Lord and the King, and meddle not with them that are given to change 24 21

13. Happy is the man that *feareth* always, but he that hardeneth his heart shall fall into mischief 28. 14.

14 The *fear* of man bringeth a snare, but whoso putteth his trust in the Lord, shall be safe 29 25

Feaſt.

1 A *Feaſt* is made for laughter, and wine maketh merry, but money anſwereth all things *Eccl.* 10 19

Fire.

1 Can a man take *fire* in his boſom, and his cloaths not be burnt ? 6 27.

Fool.

1 A *Fool* hath no delight in underſtanding; but that his heart may diſcover it ſelf. 18 2

2 *Fools* make a mock at ſin, but among the righteous there is favour. 14. 9.

3 A *Fool's* lips enter into contention, and his mouth calleth for ſtrokes 18 6.

4 A *Fools* wrath is preſently known, but a prudent man covereth ſhame. 12. 16

5. Even

8 Reverentia 2 Jehova 1 tendo ad vita, & præditus +2 + , 1s 1 maneo 14 satur, non" visitor -9 malum 19 23

9 29 Humilitas & 23 reverentia 2 Jehova 1 sum
divitiæ, & 2s honor, & 23 vita 22 4

10 5 Revereor 6 Deus & 10 observo 6 præceptum 2 1s, quia 2 hic 1 sum 2 totus officium 2 homo,
Ecclef 12 13

11 Quamvis peccator 1 facio 6 malum centies,
& dies 2 ille 1 prorogor, tamen certe 5 scio 2+ sum
bene 21 timens 21 Deus, 2 qui 9 timeo à facies 2 1s.
Eclef 8 12

12 3 Meus 26 filius 5 revereor 6 Jehova &
2 rex, nec 5 commisceo 17 ille 2 qui 9 sum 14 de-
di us 21 mutatio 24 21

13 14 Beatus 1 sum homo 3 qui 9 paveo jugi-
ter, autem 2 qui 9 obduro 3 suus 6 animus 7 ruo
in malum 28 14

14 Tremor 2 homo 1 duco 6 tendicula, autem
qui 9 confido 4 Jehova 7 sum 14 tutus. 29 25

Feaſt.

1. Convivium 1 paror ad lætitia, & vinum 1 lætifico, sed pecunia 1 respondeo 21 omnis. *Ecclef.*
10 19

Fire.

1 1 Possumne quisquam 2+ accipio 6 ignis in
si us 3 suus, nec 2 1s vestis 1 aduror 2 6 27

Fool.

1 Stolidus non 1 delector 29 intelligentia, nisi
ut 2 suus animus 1 prodo 6 sui ipse 18 2

2 Stultus 30 jocus 1 habeo 6 peccatum, sed inter rectus 1 sum benevolentia 14 9

3 2 Stolidus sermo 1 ineo 6 contentio, & 2 is os
1 advoco 6 contusio. 18 6

4 2 Stultus indignatio cito 1 agnoscor, vero
prudens 1 tego 6 ignominia 12, 16

5 Even a fool when he holdeth his peace, is counted wife, and he that ſhutteth his lips, is eſteemed a man of underſtanding 17 8.

6 It is ſport to a *fool* to do miſchief, but a man of underſtanding hath wiſdom 10 23

7 Excellent ſpeech becometh not a *fool*, much leſs do lying lips a prince 17 7

8 It is an honour for a man to ceaſe from ſtrife, but every *fool* will be meddling 20 3

9 Every prudent man dealeth with knowledge, but a *fool* layeth open his folly 13 16

10 Though thou ſhouldeſt bray a *fool* in a mortar among wheat with a peſtle, yet will not his fooliſhneſs depart from him 27 22

11 A reproof entereth more into a wiſe man, than an hundred ſtripes into a fool 17 10

12 Wherefore is there price in the hand of a *fool* to get wiſdom, ſeeing he hath no heart to it ? 17 16

13 Wiſdom is before him that hath underſtanding, but the eyes of a *fool* are in the ends of the earth. 17 24.

14 In the mouth of the *fooliſh* is a rod of pride but the lips of the wiſe ſhall preſerve them 14 3

15 Wiſdom reſteth in the heart of him that hath underſtanding, but that which is in the midſt of *fools* is made known 14 33

16 Speak not in the ears of a *fool*, for he will deſpiſe the wiſdom of thy words 23 9

17 Seeſt thou a man wiſe in his own conceit ? there is more hope of a fool than of him 26 12.

18 The crown of the wiſe is their riches, but the *fooliſhneſs* of *fools* is folly. 14 24

19 A wiſe man's heart is at his right hand, but a *fool's* heart is at his left. *Eccleſ.* 10 2.

20. The

5 Etiam ſtultus, dum [7] ſileo [1] reputor [14] ſapiens, & qui [9] obturo [6] labium [2] ſuus, [7] habeor [1] homo [5] intelligens 17 28.

6 [12] Sum [15] ludus [21] ſtolidus facio [6] ſcelus, at homo [3] intelligens [1] exerceo [6] ſapientia 10 23

7 [2] Excellens ſermo [1] deceo non [6] ſtultus, multo minus [3] mentiens labium [6] princeps. 17 7

8 [1] Sum [2] honorificus [22] vir ſuperſedeo à lis, autem [3] omnis ſtultus [1] immiſceo [6] ſui 20. 3

9 [3] Omnis prudens [1] ago cum ſcientia, autem ſtolidus [1] pando [2] ſuus [6] ſtultitia 13 16

10 Quamvis [5] contundo [6] ſtultus in mortarium cum triticum [29] piſtillum, tamen [2] is ſtultitia non [1] recedo ab [2] ipſe 27 22

11 Increpatio [1] uro magis [6] prudens, quàm centum [2] plaga [6] ſtolidus 17 10

12. Quare [1] ſum pretium in manus [2] ſtolidus ad [29] poſſideo [38] ſcientia, cum [1] deſum [25] ille animus [2] 17 16

13 Sapientia [1] ſum coram prudens, autem oculus [2] ſtolidus [1] vagor ad extremitas [2] terra 17. 24

14 [17] Os [2] ſtultus [1] inſum baculus [2] ſuperbia, vero labium [2] ſapiens [1] conſervo [6+3] ipſe 14. 3 [1]

15 Sapientia [1] requieſco in animus [2] intelligens, autem [3] qui [9] ſum in medium [2] ſtolidus [2] exhibetr [3] cognoſcendus 14 33

16.[5] Loquor ne in auditio [2] ſtolidus, nam [7] ſperno [6] prudentia [3] tuus [2] dictum 23 9

17 [5] Videone [6] vir [3] ſapiens in oculus [3] ſuus [2] [13] ſum [3] melior expectatio de ſtolidus, quam de [3] ille 26 12.

18 Corona [2] ſapiens [1] ſum [2] ille [15] divitiæ, at ſtultitia [2] ſtolidus [1] maneo [15] ſtultitia 14 24

19 Animus [2] ſapiens [1] adſum [9] ipſe [17] dextra, vero animus [2] ſtolidus [1] adſum [2] is [1] ſiniſtra *Eccleſ* 10. 2. 20 An-

20 The heart of the wife is in the houfe of mourning, but the heart of *fools* is in the houfe of mirth *Eccl f* 7 4

21 The legs of the lame are not equal, fo is a parable in the mouth of *fools* 26 7

22 As a thorn goeth up into the hand of drunkards, fo is a parable in the mouth of *fools* 26 9

23 A ftone is heavy, and the fand weighty, but a *fool's* wrath is heavier than them both 27 3.

24 As a dog returneth to his vomit, fo returneth a *fool* to his folly 26 11

25 Let a bear robbed of her whelps meet a man, rather than a *fool* in his folly 17 12

26. The words of wife men are heard in quiet, more than the cry of him that ruleth among *fools Ecclef.* 9. 17.

27 *Folly* is fet in great dignity, and the rich fit in low places *Ecclef* 10 6

28 As he that bindeth a ftone in a fling, fo is he that giveth honour unto a *fool* 26. 8

29 A whip for the horfe, a bridle for the afs, and a rod for the *fool's* back 26 3

30 He that troubleth his own houfe, fhall inherit the wind, and the *fool* fhall be fervant to the wife of heart 11. 29

31. Go from the prefence of a *foolifh* man, when thou perceiveft not in him the lips of knowledge 14 7

32 It is better to hear the rebuke of the wife, than for a man to hear the fong of *fools Ecc* 7 5.

33 He that walketh with wife men, fhall be wife, but a companion of *fools* fhall be deftroyed 13 20

34 He that fendeth a meffage by the hand of a *fool* cutteth off the feet, and drinketh damage 26 6.

35. Dead

20. Animus ² ſapiens ¹ ſum in locus ² luctus, autem animus ⁹ ſtolidus ¹ ſum in locus ² lætitia. *Eccleſ* 7 4

11 Pes ² claudus non ¹ ſum ¹⁴ æquus, ita ſum ſententia in os ² ſtolidus 26 7

22 Ut ſpina ¹ venio in manus ² ebrius, ita ¹ ſum ſententia in os ² ſtol lus 26. 9

23 Lapis ¹ ſum ¹⁴ gravis, & ²⁵ arena ³ ponde-roſus, ſed indignatio ² ſtultus ¹ ſum ¹⁴ gravier '⁵ ille ⁵ duo 27 3

24. Ut canis ¹ redeo ad ³ ſuus vomitus, ita ſtolidus ¹ redeo ad ⁵ ſuus ſtultitia 26 11

25 Urſa ³ orbatus ³ ſuus ⁴⁰ catulus ¹ occurro ¹ vii potius quam²⁵ſtolidus in ³ſuus ſtultitia 17 12

26 Verbum ⁵ ſapiens ¹ audior cum quies, po-tius quam ²³ clamor ² ille ³ qui ⁹ dominor inter ſtultus *Eccleſ* 9 17

27 Stoliditas ponor in ⁵ celſus dignitas, vero dives ¹ ſedeo in ⁵ abjectus locus *Eccleſ* 10 6

28 Ut qui ⁹ applico ⁶ lapis ¹⁷baliſta, ita ¹fa-cio ille ⁵ qui ⁹ prebeo ⁶ honor ²⁵ ſtolidus 26. 8

29 Flagellum ²¹ equus frænum ²¹ aſinus & virgo ² ſtolidus ²¹ tergum 26 3

30 Qui ⁹ conturbo ³ ſuus ⁶ domus ⁷ poſſdeo ventus & ſtultus ¹ efficior ¹³ ſervus ²¹ ſapiens, ² animus 11 29

31. ⁵ Abeo a conſpectus ³ ſtolidus ² vir quum ¹percipio non in ille ⁶ verbum ² ſcientia 14 7

32 ¹² Sum melior audio ⁶ increpto ² ſapi-ens, quam ut quis ¹ audio ⁶ canticum ² ſtolidus. *Eccl* 7 5

33 Qui ⁹ ambulo cum ſapiens, ⁷ fio ¹⁴ ſapie s, vero ſocius ² ſtolidus ¹ corrumpor 13 20

34 Qui ⁹ mitto ⁶ verbum per ſtolidus, ⁷ de-traco ⁶ pes & ¹⁵ ebibo ⁶ poena 26. 6

35 Mortuus

35 Dead flies cause the ointment of the Apothecary to send forth a stinking savour, so doth a little folly him that is in reputation for wisdom and honour, *Eccl* s 10 1

36 The wisdom of the prudent is to understand his way but the folly of *fools* is deceit 14 8

37 The great God that formed all things, both rewardeth the *fools*, and rewardeth transgressors, 26 10.

Friend.

1 He that blesseth his *friend* with a loud voice rising early in the morning, it shall be accounted unto him a curse 27* 14

2 A man that hath *friends* must shew himself friendly, and there is a *friend* that sticketh closer than a brother 18 24

3 Iron sharpeneth Iron, so doth a man sharpen the countenance of his *friend* 27 17

4 He that loveth pureness of heart, for the grace of his lips the king shall be his friend 22 11.

Froward.

1 A naughty person a wicked man, walketh with a *froward* mouth 6 12

2 He that hath a *froward* heart findeth no good; and he that hath a perverse tongue falleth into mischief 17 20

3 A *froward* man soweth strife and a whisperer separateth chief friends 16 28

4 Thorns and snares are in the way of the *froward*, he that doth keep his soul shall be far from them 22 5

5 The *froward* is abomination to the Lord, but his secret is with the righteous 3 32

6 The mouth of the just bringeth forth wisdom, but the *froward* tongue shall be cut out 10 31

7 Put away from thee a *froward* mouth, and perverse lips put far from thee. 4 24

Gift.

35 Mortuus muſca ¹ efficio ⁶ unguentum
Pharmacopola ²⁴ emitto ⁶ fœtor, ita parvus
ſtultitia ⁶ ille ³ qui ⁹ æſtimor propter ſapientia &
⁵ gloria *Eccleſ* 1⁰ 1

36 Sapientia ² aſtutus ¹² ſum intelligo ³ ſuus
via, ſed ſtultitia ² ſtolidus ¹ ſum ¹⁵ dolus 14 8

37 ⁵ Magnus ⁵ ille Deus, ⁵ qui ⁹ formo ⁶ omnis
& ⁷ compenſo ⁶ ſtultus & ¹⁰ compenſo ⁶ + ⁵ tranſ-
grediens 26. 10

Friend.

1 Qui ⁹ benedico ³ ſuis ²⁷ amicus ³ magnus
⁵ vox, ³ ſurgens tempeſtive mane, ¹² imputor
¹ maledictio ²¹ + ³ is 27 14

2 Vir ⁵ qui ⁹ habeo ⁶ amicus ¹ debeo ²⁴ præbeo ⁶ ſui ⁵ amicus, & ¹ ſum amicus ⁵ qui ⁹ hæres
¹⁴ conjunctior ¹⁵ frater 18 24

3 Ferrum ¹ acuo ⁶ ferrum, ita vir ¹ acuo ⁶ facies ⁵ ſuus ² amicus 27 7

4 Qui ⁹ amo ¹ mundities ² animus pro gratia
⁵ is ² labium Rex ¹ ſum ⁵ ille ¹⁵ amicus 22 11

Froward.

1 ⁵ Nequam homo, ⁵ improbus vir, ³⁵ ambulo
⁵ perverſus ²⁹ os 6 21

2 Qui ⁹ habeo ⁵ perverſus ⁶ animus, ⁷ conſequor ⁵ nullus ⁶ bonum & ¹¹ qui ¹ ſum ⁵ perverſus lingua ⁷ incido in malum 17, 20

3 ³ Perverſus vir ¹ immitto ⁶ conter 10, &
ſuſurro ¹ disjungo ⁵ charus ⁶ amicus 16 28.

4 Aculeus & ⁷ laqueus ⁰ ſum in via ² perverſus, qui ⁹ obſervo ⁵ ſuus ⁶ anima ⁷ ſum procul
ab is 22 ⁵

5 Perverſus ¹ ſum ¹⁷ abominatio 4⁵ Jehova,
autem arcanum ⁵ is ¹ ſum apud rectus 3 32

6 Os ² juſtus ¹ profero ⁶ ſapientia, vero ³ perverſus lingua ¹ reſcindor 10 31

7 ⁵ Removeo abs tu ⁵ perverſus ⁶ os,& ³ pravus
⁶ labium ⁵ amoveo procul abs tu 4 24

E 4   Gift.

G.

Gift.

1 A man's gift maketh room for him, and bringeth him before great men 18 16

2 A gift in secret pacifieth anger, and a reward in the bosom, strong wrath. 21 14

3. A gift is as a precious stone in the eyes of him that hath it, whithersoever it turneth, it prospereth. 17 8

4. A wicked man taketh a gift out of the bosom to pervert the ways of judgment 17 23.

5 He that is greedy of gain, troubleth his own house, but he that hateth gifts, shall live 15 27.

6 Whoso boasteth himself of a false gift, is like clouds and wind without rain 25 14

Goods.

1 When goods encrease, they are encreased that eat them, and what good is there to the owners thereof, saving the beholding of them with their eyes?

Grave.

1 Whatsoever thy hand findeth to do, do it with all thy might, for there is no work, nor device nor knowledge, nor wisdom in the grave, whither thou goest Eccles 9 10

2 There are three things that are never satisfied, yea, four things say not, It is enough, The grave and the barren womb, the earth that is not filled with water, and the fire that saith not, it is enough 30. 15 16

Hand.

1 If thou hast done foolishly in lifting up thy self, or if thou hast thought evil lay thy hand upon thy mouth 30 32

2 The king's heart is in the hand of the Lord, as the rivers of water, he turneth it whithersoever he will 21.

Hasty

Gift.

1 ² Homo donum ¹ do ⁶ acceſſus ²⁵ is, &
¹⁰ adduco ⁶+⁶ ille coram magnates 18 16

2 Donum in abditum ¹ averto ⁶ ira, & ²⁰ munus in ſinus ³ vehemens ⁶ excandeſcentia 21 14

3 Munus ¹ ſum ³ gratiſſimus ¹³ gemma in
oculus ² poſſidens ²¹+³ ille, quocunque ¹ verto,
proſpero 17 8

4 Improbus ¹ accipio ⁶ munus à ſinus ad
²⁰ perverto ⁹ iter ² jus 17 23

5 Qui ⁹ ſum ¹⁴ deditus ³¹ quæſtus ⁷ conturbo ſuus ⁶ domus, vero qui ⁹ odi ⁶ donum, ⁷ vivo ¹⁵ 27

6 Quiſquis ¹ jacto ⁶ ſui de ³ falſus don ⁿᵘᵐ,
⁷ ſum velut ²³ vapor & ²⁰ ventus ſine pluvia 25 ¹⁴·

Goods.

1 Cum bonum ¹ augeo, ² ille ¹ multiplico ² qui
comedo ⁶+² ille, ergo ² quis commodum ¹ ſum
³ dominus, præterquam ²⁰ aſpectus ² is cum
ſuus oculus ?

Grave.

6 + Quiſquis ² tuus manus ¹ aſſequor ut ⁵ facio,
facio pro ² tuus facultas, nam ¹ ſum ² nullus opus,
e ²³ excogitatio nec ²⁻ ſcientia nec ²³ ſapientia
in ſepulcrum quo ⁵ eo Eccleſ 9 10.

² Sum tres qui nunquam ⁹ ſatior imo quatuor ⁷ dico non ²⁴ ſum ſatis, ſepulcrum & oc-
cluſus ²³ uterus, terra qui non ⁹ ſatior ⁹ aqua
& ignis ³ qui ⁹ dico non ²⁴ ſum ſatis. 30 15. 16

Hand.

1 Si ⁵ facio ſtulte ³⁸ effero ⁷⁹ tu, aut ſi ⁵ cogito ⁶ malum ⁵ impono ³ tuus ⁶ manus ² tuus
os 30 3

2 Rex animus ¹ ſum in manus ² Jehova, ut
rivus ² aqua; ⁷ inclino ⁶+⁴ is quocunque ⁷ volo. 23. 1.

Hasty.

1 Seeſt thou a man that is *haſty* in his words? there is more hope of a fool, than of him 29 20.

2 He that is ſlow to wrath is of great underſtanding, but he that is *haſty* of ſpirit, exalteth folly 4 29

3 Go not forth *haſtily* to ſtrive, leſt thou know not what to do in the end thereof, when thy neighbour hath put thee to ſhame 25 8.

4 Be not raſh with thy mouth, and let not thy heart be *haſty* to utter any thing before God, for God is in heaven, and thou upon earth, therefore let thy words be few. *Eccl.* 5 2

Hatred.

1 *Hatred* ſtirreth up ſtrife, but love covereth all ſins 10 12

2 He that hideth *hatred* with lying lips, and he that uttereth a ſlander, is a fool 10 18

3 Better is a dinner of herbs, where love is, than a ſtalled ox, and *hatred* therewith 15. 17

Head.

1 Let thy garments be always white, and let thy *head* lack no ointment *Eccl.* 9 8

2 The glory of young men is their ſtrength, and the beauty of old men is their grey head. 20 29

3 The hoary *head* is a crown of glory, if it be found in the way of righteouſneſs. 16 31.

Heart.

1 My ſon give me thy *heart*, and let thine eyes obſerve my ways 23 26.

2 A man's *heart* deviſeth his way, but the Lord directeth his ſteps 16 9

3 The *heart* knoweth its own bitterneſs, and a ſtranger doth not intermeddle with his joy.

Hasty.

1 · Videone ⁶ vir q ᵢ ⁵ fum ¹⁴ præceps in ᵎ fuus verbum ? ᵎ fum ¹⁴ melior expectatio de ſtolidus, quam de ᵎ ille 29 20

2 Qui ⁹ fum tardu, ad ira ⁷ fum ᵎ magnus ᵎ⁰ intelligentia, autem qui ⁹ fum ¹⁴ præceps ¹⁸ animus, ⁷ excito ⁶ ſtul ᵢ ia 14 9

3 Ne ⁵ proleo feſtinanter ad ᵎ⁹ litigo, ne ⁵ ignoro ⁶ quis ⁵ facio tandem, quum ³ tuus proximus ᵎ adduco ⁶ tu ad ignominia 25 8

4 Ne ⁵ accelero ᵎ tuus ⁹ᵎ os & ne tu animus ᵎ teſtino ᵎᵎ profero ⁶ quiſquam coram Deus, ᵢum Deus ᵎ fum in cælum, & ²ᵎ tu ſuper terra, idᵎᵎᵎ tuus verbum ᵎ fum ¹⁴ paucus *Ecclef* 5. 2.

Hatred.

1 Odium ᵎ excito ⁶ contentio, vero charitas ᵎ obrego ᵎ omnis ⁶ defectio 10 12

2 Qui ⁹ tego ⁶ odium ₃ fallax ²⁹ labium, & qui ⁹ profero ⁶ infamia, fum ¹⁵ ſtolidus ᵢᵎ 18

3 ᵎᵎ Melior ᵎ fum c barium ² olus, ubi ᵎ fum dilectio, quam faginatus ²ᵎ bos, & ²ᵎ odium cum ᵎ ille. 15 17

Head.

1 ᵎ Tuus veſtimentum ᵎ fum femper ᵎᵎ nitidus, & ᵎ tuus caput ᵎ careo ᵎe ⁶ unguentum *E*ᵎ 9 8.

2 Ornamentum ᵎ vivens ᵎ fum ᵎᵎᵎ ille ¹ᵎ vis, & decor ² ſenex ᵎ fum ¹ᵎ canities 20 29

3 Canities ᵎ fum ¹ᵎ corona ² gloria, ſi ᵎ invenior in via ᵎ juſtitia 16 31

Heart.

1 ₃ Meus ²ᵎ filius ⁵ dᵎ ᵎ⁵ ᵎ tuus ⁶ cor, & ᵎ tuus oculus ᵎ obſe vo ³ meus ⁶ via 23 26

2 ² Homo animus ᵎ excogito ³ fuus ⁶ via, ſed Jehova ᵎ ſtatuo ²ille ⁶ greſſus 16 9

3 Animus ᵎ cognoſco ³ fuus ⁶ amaritudo, & extraneus non ᵎ intermiſceo ⁶ ſui in ²ᵢs læ ᵢtia. 14 10.

4 ᵎ Lætus

H

4 A merry heart maketh a chearful countenance. but by sorrow of the *heart* the spirit is
broken 15 13

5. A merry *heart* doth good like a medicine
but a broken spirit drieth the bones 17 22

6 It is beter to go into the house of mourning, than to go to the house of feasting, for that
is the end of all men, and the living will lay it
to hart Eccl. 7 2

7 As he that taketh away a garment in cold
weather, and as vinegar upon nitre, so is he
that singeth songs to an heavy *heart* 25 20

8 The foolishnefs of man peverteth his way,
and his *heart* fretteth against the Lord 19 3

9 The *heart* of him that hath underſtanding
ſeeketh knowledge, but the mouth of fools
feedeth on foolishnefs 15 14

10 The tongue of the juſt is as choice ſilver,
the *heart* of the wicked is little worth

11 He that truſteth in his own *heart*, is a fool,
or whoſo walketh wiſely, he ſhall be delivered
28 26

12 The heaven for height, and the earth for
depth, and the *heart* of kings is unſearchable
25 3.

13 The fining pot is for ſilver, and the furnace for gold, but the Lord trieth the heart
17 3

14 Hell and deſtruction are before the Lord;
how much more then the *hearts* of the children
of men ? 15 11

15 As in water face anſwereth to face, so the
heart of man to man 27 19

16 Who can ſay, I have made my *heart* clean,
I am pure from ſin ? 20 9

Honey.

4 ³Lætus animus ¹facio ²lætus ⁶vultus, at ⁷dolor ²animus ⁶spiritus ¹frangor 15 13

5 ³Lætus animus ¹benefacio ²⁵tanquam medicina, autem ³fractus spiritus ¹exsicco ⁶os 17 22

6 ¹⁻Sum ¹⁴melior adeo ⁶locus ²luctus, quam ⁷adeo ⁶locus ²convivium, nam ⁷ille ¹sum ⁷finis ³omnis ²homo, & vivens ¹indo ⁶ille ⁵suus ¹⁷animus *Ecclef.* 7 2

7 Ut qui ⁹eripio ⁶vestis in tempus ²frigus, & ⁷ï acetum ⁵per nitrum ita ⁷sum qui ⁹cano ⁶canticum apud male ³affectus animus 25 20

8 Stultitia ²homo ¹perverto ⁴ipse ⁶os & ²is animus ¹indignor adversus Jehova 19 3

9 Animus ²prudens ¹quæro ⁶scientia, autem os ²stolidus ¹pascor ⁴⁷stultitia 15 14.

10 Lingua ²justus ¹sum ut ²lectissimus ²³argentum, animus ²improbus ¹sum ⁴⁸perparvus.

11 Qui ⁹confido ⁵suus ⁴animus ⁷sum ¹stultus, autem qui ⁹ambulo sapienter is ¹eripior 28 26.

12 Cœlum ⁴⁹altitudo & ²³terra ⁴⁹profunditas & ²³animus ²rex ¹sum ⁷⁴inscrutabilis. 25 3

13 ³Fusorius vas ¹adhibeor ¹⁷argentum, & ⁷catinus ²³aurum, at Jehova ¹probo ⁶cor. 17 3

14 Infernus & ²³perditio ³⁰sum coram Jehova, quanto magis igitur animus ⁻filius ²homo? 15 11

15 Ut in aqua ¹facies ¹observor ⁻⁹facies, ita animus ²homo ²⁹homo 27 19

16 Quis ¹possum ²⁴dico, ⁵purifico ³meus ⁶animus, ⁵sum ¹⁴mundus à ³meus peccatum? 20. 9.

Honey.

1 Haſt thou found *honey?* eat ſo much as is ſufficie t for thee, leſt thou be filled therewith, and vomit it 5 16

Honour.

1. He that followeth after righteouſneſs and mercy, findeth life, righteouſneſs and *honour* 21. 21

2. A gracious woman retaineth *honour*, and ſtrong men retain riches 11 16

3 A man's pride ſhall bring him low, but *honour* ſhall uphold the humble in ſpirit 19 23

4 Whoſo keepeth the fig-tree, ſhall eat the fruit thereof, ſo he that waiteth on his maſter ſhall be *honoured* 27 18.

5 In the multitude of the people is the king's *honour*, but in the want of the people is the deſtruction of the prince 14 28

6 As ſnow in ſummer, and as rain in harveſt, ſo *honour* is not ſeemly for a fool 26 1.

Hope.

1 *Hope* deferred maketh the heart ſick, but when the deſire cometh, it is a tree of life 13 12.

2 To him that is joined to all the living there is *hope*, for a living dog is better than a dead Lion *Eccleſ* 9 4.

3. The *hope* of the righteous ſhall be gladneſs, but the expectation of the wicked ſhall periſh 10 28

4 When a wicked man dieth, his expectation ſhall periſh, and the *hope* of unjuſt men periſheth 11 7

Houſe.

1 The *Houſe* of the wicked ſhall be overthrown, but the tabernacle of the upright ſhall flouriſh. 14. 11.

2, The

Honey.

1 ^{5} Invenio ^{6} mel $^?$ comedo qui $^?$ sum satis
tu, ne ^{5} saturor ^{29}+ is, & ^{10} evomo ^{6}+ ille.
25 16.

Honour.

1 Qui ^{9} sector ^{6} justitia & ^{2} benignitas, ^{7} consequor ^{6} vita, ^{6} justitia & ^{2} honor 21. 21

2 ^{9} Gratiosus mulier ^{1} contineo ^{6} honor, &
potens ^{1} contineo ^{6} divitiæ 11 16

3 ^{2} Homo elatio ^{1} deprimo ^{6}+$^?$ is, autem honor ^{1} sustento ^{6} depressus $^{3?}$ spiritus 29 23

4 Qui ^{9} custodio ^{6} ficus ^{7} con edo ^{6} fructus
^{2} ille ita qui ^{9} observor ^{3} suus ^{6} dominus, ^{7} honorer 27 18.

5 In multitudo ^{2} populus ^{1} sum ^{2} rex decus,
at in defectus ^{2} ratio ^{1} sum contritio ^{2} dominator 14. 28

6 Ut nix in æstas, & ut pluvia in messis, ita
honor non ^{1} convenio ^{17} stultus 26 1.

Hope.

1 Spes ^{3} protractus ^{1} efficio ^{6} animus ^{3} æger,
autem cum desider um ^{1} advenio, ^{1} sum ^{13} arbor ^{2} vita 13 12.

2 ^{45} Is qui ^{9} associor ^{3} omnis ^{17} vivens ^{1} sum
spes, quippe ^{3} vivens canis ^{1} sum ^{14} melior
^{3} mortuus ^{15} leo *Eccles* 9. 4.

3 Spes ^{2} justus ^{1} sum ^{15} lætitia, vero expectatio ^{2} improbus ^{1} pereo. 10. 28

4 Cum ^{3} improbus homo ^{1} morior, ^{2} is expectatio ^{1} pereo, etiam spes ^{2} injustus ^{1} pereo.
11. 7.

House.

1. Domus ^{2} improbus ^{1} perdor, autem tentorium ^{2} rectus ^{1} floreo. 14. 11.

2. Jehova

2 The Lord will deſtroy the *houſe* of the proud, but he will eſtabliſh the border of the widow 15 25

3 The wicked are overthrown, and are not, but the *houſe* of the righteous ſhall ſtand 1: 7

4 In the *houſe* of the righteous is much treaſure, but in the revenues of the wicked is trouble 15 6

5 Through wiſdom is an *houſe* builded, and by underſtanding it s eſtabliſhed 24 3.

6. Withdraw thy foot from thy neighbour's *houſe*, leſt he be weary of thee, and ſo hate thee 25 17

Humble.

1 Better it is to be of an *humbl* ſpirit with the lowly, than to divide the ſpoil with the proud 16 19

2 Do this now my Son, and deliver thy ſelf, when thou art come into the hand of thy friend, ſo *humble* thy ſelf, and make ſure of thy friend. 6 3.

Hunger.

1 Slothfulneſs caſteth into a deep ſleep, and an idle ſoul ſhall ſuffer *hunger* 19 5

2 Men do not deſpiſe a thief, if he ſteal to ſatisfie his ſoul, when he is *hungry* 6 30

3 The full ſoul loatheth the honey-comb, but to the *hungry* ſoul every bitter thing is ſweet. 27 7

Hypocrite.

1 An *hypocrite* with his mouth deſtroyeth his neighbour, but through knowledge ſhall the juſt be delivered 11 9

Increaſe.

1 Honour the Lord with thy ſubſtance, and with the firſt-fruits of all thy *increaſe*. 3. 9

2 There

2 Jehova ¹ evello ⁶ domus ² superbus, autem constituo ⁶ terminus ² vidua 15 25

3 Improbus ¹ evertor, nec ⁷ sum , autem fami-lia ² justus ¹ sto 12. 7.

4 In domus ⁷ justus ¹ sum ³ multus opes, at in proventus ² improbus ¹ sum perturbatio 15 6

5 ²⁵ Sapientia domus ¹ ædificor, & ²⁹ intelligen-tia ¹⁰ stabilio 24 3

6 ⁵ Contineo ³ tuus ⁶ pes à ⁵ tuus ² proximus domus, ne ⁷ saturor ⁸ tu, ac ita ⁵⁰ odium ¹⁰ habeo ⁶ tu 25 7

Humble.

1 ¹⁴ Melior ¹² sum sum ⁵ submissus ³⁷ spiritus cum mansuetus, quam ¹⁰ partior ⁶ spolium cum superbus 16. 19

2 ⁵ Facio ⁶ iste jam ⁵ meus ²⁰ filius & ¹⁰ eripio ⁶ u, quando convenio in manus ⁵ tuus ⁴proximus; ⁶ ago ⁵ subjicio ⁶ tu & ¹⁰ interpello ³ tuus ⁶ prox-imus 6 3.

Hunger.

1 Pigritia ¹ injicio ⁵ altus ⁶ sopor, & ³ igna-vus anima ¹ esurio 19 15

2 Homo ¹ contemno non ⁶ fur, si ⁷ furor ad ⁵ expleo ⁵ suus ²⁹ animus cum ⁷ esurio 6 30

3 ³ Satur animus ¹ calco ⁶ favus, vero ⁵ fame-licus ²² anima ⁵ omnis amarus ¹ ium ¹⁴ dulcis 27 7

Hypocrite.

1 Hypocrita ³ suus ²⁵ os ¹ corrumpo ⁵ suus ⁶ proximus, at ²⁹ scientia justus ¹ liberor 11 9.

Increase.

1. ⁵ Honoro ⁶Jehova de ⁵ tuus substantia, & de primitiæ ³ totus ⁵ tuus ² proventus 3 9

2 Sum

2 There is that scattereth, and yet *incr afet*, and there is that with-holden more than is meet, but it tendeth to poverty 11 24

Inheritance.

1. Wisdom is good with an *inheritance* and by it there is profit to them that see the Sun *Ec* 7 11.

2 A good man leaveth an *inheritance* to his childrens children, and the wealth of the wicked is laid up for the just 13 22

3 An *inheritance* may be gotten hastily in the beginning, but the end thereof shall not be blessed 20 1

Instruction.

1 Apply thy heart unto *instruction*, and thine ears to the word of knowledge 23 12

2. Hear *instruction*, and be wise, and refuse it not. 8 33

3 Whoso loveth *instruction*, loveth knowledge, but he that hateth reproof is brutish 12 1

4 He is in the way of life that keepeth *instruction*, but he that hateth reproof erreth 10 17

5 The Commandment is a lamp and the law is light, and reproofs of *instruction* are the way of life 6 23.

6 Give *instruction* to a wife man, and he will be yet wiser, teach a just man and he will increase in learning 9 9

7 He that refuseth *instruction*, despiseth his own soul, but he that heareth reproof, getteth understanding

8 Poverty and shame shall be to him that refuseth *instruction*, but he that regardeth reproof shall be honoured 13 18.

9 Take fast hold of *instruction* let her not go, keep her, for she is thy life 4 13

10 Cea*se*

2 ⁷Sum qui ⁹difpergo, tamen ⁷augeo, &
¹⁰fum qui ⁹cohibeo plus ¹⁵æquus, at ¹²tendo ad
egeſtas 11 24

Inheritance.

1. Sapientia ¹fum ¹⁴bonus cum poſſeſſio, &
per ²15 ¹fum emolumentum ⁴⁵aſpiciens ³¹Sol.
to leſ 7 11

2 Bonus ¹trado ⁶poſſeſſio ³fuus ²filius ²⁵fili-
us, & opes peccator ¹recondor ²¹juſtus 13 22.

3. Poſſeſſio ¹poſſum ²⁴acquiror feſtinanter in
principium, autem finis ²ille non ¹benedicor
20 21

Inſtruction.

1 ⁵Adhibeo ²tuus ⁶animus ad eruditio, &
tuus ²⁰auris ad ſermo ²ſcientia 23

2 ⁵Audio ⁶eruditio & ¹⁰ſapio, & ne ¹⁰reſ-
puo ⁶+³ille 8. 33

3 Qui ⁹amo ⁶eruditio, ⁷amo ⁶ſcientia , vero qui ⁹odi ⁶correptio, ⁷fum ¹⁴brutus 12 1

4 ⁷Sum in iter ²vita qui ⁹ſervo ⁶eruditio,
vero qui ⁹derelinquo ⁶correptio ⁷erro 10 17

5 Præceptum ¹fum ¹⁵lucerna, & doctrina
¹fum ⁵lux, & correctio ²eruditio ¹fum ¹³via
-vita 6 23

6 ⁵Do ⁶eruditio ²⁵ſapiens & amplius ⁷ſapio,
⁵doceo ⁶juſtus & ⁷creſco ſub doctrina 9 9.

7 Qui ⁹nolo ⁶eruditio ⁷ſperno ³ſuus ⁶ani-
ma, autem qui ⁹auſculto ⁶correptio ⁷poſſideo
⁶intelligentia

8. Paupertas & ²³ignominia ²⁰fum ⁴⁵recu-
ſans ³¹eruditio, autem qui ⁹ſervo ⁶correptio ⁷ho-
noror 13 18

9 ⁵Prehendo ⁶eruditio, ne ⁵dimitto ⁶+³il-
le, ⁵cuſtodio ⁶+²ille, quia ¹fum ³tuus ¹⁵vita.
4 13.

10. ⁵Deſi 10

10 Ceaſe my ſon to hear the inſtruction, that cauſeth to err from the words of knowledge 19 27.

Integrity.

1 The *integrity* of the upright ſhall guide them, but the perverſeneſs of tranſgreſſors ſhall deſtroy them 11 13

2 Better is the poor that walketh in his *integrity*, than he that is perverſe in his lips and is a fool. 19 1

Judgment.

1 The king by *judgment* eſtabliſheth the land, but he that receiveth gifts. overthroweth it 29 4

2 Many ſeek the rulers favour, but every man's *judgment* cometh from the Lord. 29 26

3. Much food is in the tillage of the poor, but there is that is deſtroyed for want of *judgment* 13 23

4 Whoſo keepeth the commandment ſhall feel no evil thing and a wiſe man's heart diſcerneth both time and *judgment* Eccl. 8 5

5 Becauſe to every purpoſe there is time and *judgment*, therefore the miſery of man is great upon him 8 6

6 The robbery of the wicked ſhall deſtroy them, becauſe they refuſe to do *judgment* 21 7

7 *Judgments* are prepared for ſcorners, and ſtripes for the back of fools 19 29

Juſt.

1 It is joy to the *juſt* to do judgment, but deſtruction ſhall be to the workers of iniquity 21 15

2 The *juſt* man walketh in his integrity, his children are bleſſed after him 20 7

3 The path of the *juſt* is as the ſhining light, that ſhineth more and more unto the perfect day. 4 18

10 ⁵ Defino ⁵ meus ²⁶ filius ²⁴ aufculto ⁶ eruditio, ⁷ qui ⁹ facio ⁻⁴ aberro a fereno⁵ᵗ Scientia 19 7

Integrity.

1 Integrit s ⁻ rectus ¹ deduco ⁶+⁷ is, at perverfitas ⁻ perficiofus ¹ devafto ⁶+⁷ is 11 13

2 ¹⁷ Melior ¹ fum pauper ⁷ qui ⁹ ambulo in fuus integritas, ¹⁵ ille qui ⁹ fum ¹⁴ perverfus fuus labium & ⁶ fum ¹⁵ folidus 19 1.

Judgment.

1 Rex ²⁹ judicium ¹ ftabilio ⁶ regio, vero qui ⁷ accipio ⁶ munus ⁷ deftruo ⁶+⁷ is ⁷9 4.

2 Multus ¹ quæro ² dominans ⁶ favor, verum ⁻ unufquifque jus ¹ fum a Jehova 29 26

3 ⁷ Multus cibus ¹ fum in cultura ² pauper, fed ⁷ fum qui ⁷ confumor præ inopia ² judicium. 13 23

4 Qui ⁹ obfervo ⁶ præceptum, ⁷ experior non ⁵ malus ⁶ res, & ⁷ fapiens animus) ⁵ nofco & ⁶ tempus & ⁻⁷ ratio *Ecclef* 8 5

5 Quoniam ³ quifque ⁴⁵ voluntas ¹ fum tempus & ²⁷ ratio, ideo miferia ² homo ¹ fum ¹⁴ magnus ⁴⁵ ille. 8 6

6 Vaftitas ² improbus ¹ diffeco ⁶+⁵ ipfe, quia ⁷ renuo ²⁴ exerceo ⁶ jus 21. 7

7. Judicium ¹ paror in derifor, & ²⁷ contufi in tergum ² folidus 19

Juft.

1. ¹² Sum ¹³ lætitia ⁴⁵ juftus facio ⁶ jus, vero contritio ¹ fum ⁴⁵ operarius ² iniquitas 21. 15.

2 Juftus ¹ ambulo in ⁷ fuus integritas, ² ille filius ¹ fum ¹⁴ beatus poft ⁵ is. 20. 7.

3 Iter ² juftus ¹ fum ¹⁴ fimilis ³ fplendidus ²⁻ lux, ⁵ qui ⁹ luceo magis magifque ufque ad ⁷ perfectus dies 4. 18.

4. Memoria

4 The memory of the *juſt* is bleſſed, but the name of the wicked ſhall rot 10 7.

5 The wicked is ſnared by the tranſgreſſion of his lips, but the *juſt* ſhall come out of trouble 12 13

6 A *juſt* man falleth ſeven times, and riſeth up again, but the wicked ſhall fall into miſchief

7 He that juſtifieth the wicked, and he that condemneth the *juſt*, even they both are an abomination to the Lord 17 15

8 To puniſh the *juſt* is not good, nor to ſtrike Princes for equity 17 26

King.

1 A Divine Sentence is in the lips of the *king*, his mouth tranſgreſſeth not in judgment 16. 10

2 It is an abomination to *kings* to commit wickedneſs, for the throne is eſtabliſhed by righteouſneſs 16 12

3 Righteous lips are the delight of *kings*, and they love him that ſpeaketh right 16 13

4 A *king* that ſitteth in the throne of judgment, ſcattereth away all evil with his eyes 20. 8

5 A wiſe *king* ſcattereth the wicked, and bringeth the wheel over them 20 26

6 It is the glory of God to conceal a thing, but the honour of *kings* is to ſearch out a matter. 25 2,

7 Where the word of a *king* is there is power, and who may ſay unto him, What doeſt thou? *Eccleſ* 8 4

8 The wrath of a *king* is a meſſenger of death, but a wiſe man will pacifie it 16 14

9. The *king's* wrath is as the roaring of a lion, but his favour is as dew upon the graſs 19 12.

10 In the light of the *king's* countenance is life, and his favour is as a cloud of the latter rain. 16. 15.　　　　　　　11. The

4 Memoria ² justus · sum ·¹ benedictus, autem nomen - improbus ¹ putresco ¹⁰ 7

5 Improbus ¹ irretior a defectio ² suus ² labium, ut justus ¹ egredior ab angustia 12 13

6 Justus ¹ cado septies, & ¹⁰ exurgo rursus,
vero improbus ¹ corruo in malum 24 16

7 Qui ⁹ absolvo ⁶ improbus, & qui ⁹ condemno
⁵ justus, æque ²⁰ ambo ¹ sum ¹ abominatio ¹⁵ Jehova ¹7 15

8 Multo ⁶ justus non ¹² sum ¹⁴ bonus, nec
percutio ⁶ Princeps propter æquitas ¹7 26

King.

1 ³ Divinus sententia ¹ insideo ¹ labium ²Rex.
-is os non ¹ prævaricor in judicium 16 10

2 ¹² sum ¹⁵ abominatio ⁴⁵ Rex committo ⁶ improbitas, nam solium ¹ stabilior -⁹ justitia. 16. 12.

3 ³ Justus labium ¹ sum ¹³ deliciæ ²Rex, &
-diligo ⁶ loquens ¹ rectum 16 13

4 Rex ² insidens ²¹ solium ² judicium, ¹ ventilo ² omnis ⁶ malum ³ suus ²⁹ oculus ²⁰. 8

5 ² Sapiens Rex ¹ ventilo ⁶ improbus &
- converto ⁶ rota in ³ ille 20 26

6 ¹· Sum ¹³ honor ² Deus abscondo ⁶ res, autem honor ² Rex ¹ sum pervestigo ⁶ res. 25. 2.

7 Ubicunque verbum ² Rex ¹ sum, ibi ¹ sum
dominatio, & ecquis ¹ dico ¹⁶ ille, ⁶ Quis ⁵ facio ? *Ecclef* 8 4.

8 Excandescentia ² Rex ¹ sum ut ²⁵ nuntius
-mors, sed ² sapiens vir ¹ mollio ⁶ + ² is 16 14.

9 · Rex indignatio ¹ sum ut ²⁵ rugitus ² leo,
autem ² is benevolentia ¹ sum ut ²³ ros super
herba 19 12.

10 In lux ² Rex ² facies ¹ sum vita, & ² is
benevolentia ¹ sum veluti ²⁵ nubes ³ serotinus
- pluvia. 16. 15.   Rex

11 The *king* that faithfully judgeth the poor, his throne shall be established for ever   29 14

12 Wo to thee, O Land, when thy *king* is a child, and thy princes eat in the morning *Eccle* 10 16

13 Take away the wicked from before the *king*, and his throne shall be established in righteousness   25. 5

14 Curse not the *king*, no not in thy thought, and curse not the rich in thy bed-chamber, for a bird of the air shall carry the voice, and that which hath wings shall tell the matter, *Ec* 10. 20

Knowledge.

1 There is gold and a multitude of rubies, but the lips of *knowledge* are a precious jewel 20 15

2. Receive my instruction, and not silver, and *knowledge* rather than choice gold   8 10

3 That the soul be without *knowledge* it is not good, and he that hasteth with his feet, sinneth. 19 22

4 He that hath *knowledge*, spareth his words, and a man of understanding is of an excellent spirit 17 29

5 Wisdom is a defence, and Money is a defence, but the excellency of *knowledge* is that Wisdom giveth life to them that have it *Ecclef* 7. 12.

Labour.

1 In all *Labour* there is a profit; but the talk of the lips tendeth only to penury. 14 23

2 He that *laboureth*, laboureth for himself, for his mouth craveth it of him   16 26

3 All the *labour* of man is for his mouth, and yet the appetite is not filled *Ecclef* 6 7

4 Wealth gotten by vanity, shall be diminished, but he that gathereth by *labour*, shall increase. 13. 11.

5 There

11 Rex 3 qui fideliter 9 judico 6 pauper, 4 + 3 ipfe folium 1 ftabilior in perpetuum 29. 14.

12 Hei 51 tu 26 Regio cum 3 tuus Rex 1 fum 15 puer & 3 tuus Princeps 1 comedo mane *Eccl.* 10 16

13 5 Aufero 6 improbus a confpectus 2 Rex, & 3 + 3 is folium ftabilior 29 juftitia 25 5

14 Ne 5 maledico 11 Rex, ne quidem in 3 tuus animus & ne 5 maledico 11 dives in 3 tuus conclave, nam avis 2 coelum 1 perfero 6 vox, & ales 1 ind co 6 verbum *Ecclef* 10 20

Knowledge.

1 1 Sum aurum & 23 copia 2 carbunculus; at labium 2 fcientia 11 fum pretiofus 15 gemma 20 15

2 5 Accipio 3 meus 6 eruditio 3c non 33 pecunia, & 23 fcientia potius quam 3 lectiffimus - aurum 8 10

3 Ut animus 1 careo 8 fcientia non 11 fum - bonus, & qui 3 propero 3 fuus 29 pes, 3 pecco. 19 22

4 Vir qui 9 poffideo 6 fcientia, 1 cohibeo 2 fuus 6 fermo, & vir 3 intelligens 1 fum 3 eximius 15 fpiritus 17 29

5 Sapientia 1 fum 13 umbra, & pecunia 1 fum 1 umbra, fed excellentia 2 fcientia 1 fum, quod fapientia 1 confero 6 vita - 1 poffeffor *Ecclef* 7 12.

Labour.

1. In 3 omnis labor 1 fum emolumentum, at verbum 2 labium 1 tendo tantum ad egeftas 24 23

2 Qui 9 laboro, 7 laboro - 1 fui, nam - 1s os 110 1 6 hic ab ille 16 26

3 3 Omnis labor 2 homo 1 obvenio 3 ipfe 7 os, nen defiderium non 1 expleo *Eccl.* 6 7.

4 Subftantia 3 acquifitus ex vanitas 1 diminuor, autem qui 9 congrego - 1 manus 7 augeo 13 11

11 The *king* that faithfully judgeth the poo his throne shall be established for ever 29 14

12 Wo to thee, O Land, when thy *king* is a child, and thy princes eat in the morning *Eccl* 10 16

13 Take away the wicked from before the *king*, and his throne shall be established in right-ousness 25 5

14 Curse not the *king*, no not in thy thought, and curse not the rich in thy bed-chamber, for a bird of the air shall carry the voice, and that which hath wings shall tell the matter, *Ec* 10. 20

Knowledge.

1. There is gold and a multitude of rubies, but the lips of *knowledge* are a precious jewel 20 15

2. Receive my instruction, and not silver, and *knowledge* rather than choice gold 8 10

3 That the soul be without *knowledge* it is not good, and he that hasteth with his feet, sinneth 19 22.

4 He that hath *knowledge*, spareth his words, and a man of understanding is of an excellent spirit 17 19

5 Wisdom is a defence, and Money is a defence, but the excellency of *knowledge* is that Wisdom giveth life to them that have it *Ecclef.* 7 12.

Labour.

1 In all *Labour* there is a profit; but the talk of the lips tendeth only to penury. 14 23

2 He that *laboureth*, laboureth for himself, for his mouth craveth it of him 16 26

3 All the *labour* of man is for his mouth, and yet the appetite is not filled *Ecclef* 6 7

4. Wealth gotten by vanity, shall be diminished, but he that gathereth by *labour*, shall increase. 13. 11.

5. There

11 Rex ⁊ qui fideliter 9 judico 6 pauper,
ᵃ⁺ˀ ipfe folium ¹ ſtabilior in perpetuum 29 14.

2 Hei ⁵¹ tu ²⁶ Regio cum ³ tuus Rex ¹ ſum
¹ puer, & ⁊ tuus Princeps ¹ comedo mane. *Eccl* ſ
10 16

13 ⁵ Aufero ⁶ improbus a conſpectus ² Rex, &
²⁺ is folium ſtabilior ²⁹ juſtitia 25 5

14 Ne ⁵ maledico ¹ʳ Rex, ne quidem in ³ tuus
inimus & ne ⁵ maledico ¹ dives in ³ tuus conclave, nam a⁊ s ² coelum ¹ perfero ⁶ vox, & ales-
ᵒⁿd co ⁶ verbum *Ecclef* 10 20.

Knowledge.

1 ¹ Sum aurum & ⁊ copia ² carbunculus, at
²ⁱⁿʳᵘm ² ſcientia ¹ʳ ſum pretiofus ¹⁵ gemma 20 15.

2 ⁵ Accipio ³ meus ⁶ eruditio ⁊c non ⁊ pecunia, & ²⁊ ſcientia potius quam ³ lectiſſimus ⁊ aurum 8 10

3 Ut animus ¹ careo ⁸ ſcientia non ¹ ſum
⁊ bonus, & qui ⁊ propero ³ ſuus ²⁹ pes, ⁊ pecco
9 22

4 Vir qui ⁹ poſſideo ⁶ ſcientia, ¹ cohibeo ² ſuus ⁶ ſermo, & vir intelligens ¹ ſum ⁊ eximius
¹⁵ ſpiritus 17 29

5 Sapientia ¹ ſum ¹³ umbra, & pecun a ¹ ſum
¹ umbra, ſed excellentia ⁊ ſcientia ¹ ſum, quod
ſapientia ¹ confero ⁶ vita ²¹ poſſeſſor *Ecclef* 7 12.

Labour.

1. In ³ omnis labor ¹ ſum emolumentum, at
verbum ² labium ¹ tendo tantum ad egeſt s 24 23

2 Qui ⁹ laboro, ⁷ laboro ²¹ ſui, nam ⁊ is os ⁊ʳ⁰
go ⁶ hic ab ille 16 26

3 ⁊ Omnis labor ² homo ¹ obvenio ⁊ ipſe ⁷ os,
tamen deſiderium non expleo *Ecclef* 6 7

4 Subſtantia ³ acquiſitus ex ⁊ nitas ¹ diminuor,
autem qui ⁹ congrego ⁊ manus ⁊ augeo 13 11

5 There is a man whofe *labour* is in wifdom, and in knowledge, and in equity, yet to a man that hath not *laboured* therein, fhall he leave it for his portion. *Ecclef* 2 21

6 There is nothing better for a man, than that he fhou'd eat and drink, and that he fhould make his foul enjoy good in his labour *Ecclef* 2 24

7 Every man alfo to whom God hath given riches and wealth, and hath given him power to eat thereof, and to take his portion, and to rejoice in his *labour*, this is the gift of God *Eccl f* 5 19

8 What hath a man of all his *labour*, and of the vexation of his heart, wherein he hath *laboured under* the Sun? *Ecclef* 2 22

9 As he came forth of his Mother's Womb, naked fhall he return to go as he came, and fhall take nothing of his *labour* which he may carry away in his hand *Eccl.* 5 15

10 This is alfo a fore evil, that in all points as he came fo fhall he go, and what profit hath he, that hath *laboured* for the wind? *Ecclef.* 5 16

Land.

1 He that tilleth his *land* fhall have plenty of bread but he that followeth after vain perfons, fhall have poverty enough 28 19

2 Remove not the ancient *Land mark*, which thy Fathers have fet 22 28

3 For the tranfgreffion of a *Land*, many are the princes thereof, but by a man of underftanding and knowledge, the ftate thereof fhall be prolong'd 28 2

Laughter.

1 Even in *laughter* the heart is forrowful, and the end of that mirth is heavinefs. 14 13

2 I faid of *laughter*, it is mad, and of mirth, what doth it? *Ecclef* 2. 2.

3. Sor-

5 ¹Sum homo ²qui labor ¹conficio ²⁹ſapi-
entia, & ²ˈſcientia, & ²ˈæquitas, autem ²⁵homo
qui non ⁹laboro in   ille trado ⁶+ˈille in ²ille
pars. *Eccleſ* 2 21

6 ¹Sum nil ¹⁴melior ²²homo quam ut ⁷co-
medo & ¹⁰bibo, & ut ¹⁰efficio ³ſuus ⁶animus
²⁴fruor ⁴⁷bonum ex ³ſuus labor *Eccleſ.* 2. 24

7 Unuſquiſque etiam ²⁵qui Deus ¹do ⁶divi-
tiæ, &ˍ²³facultas, & ¹⁰facio ²⁵is ⁶copia ⁵²come-
do ex ³ille, & ⁵²percipio ³ſuus ³⁹pars, ac ⁵²læ-
tor de ³ſuus labor, ³hic ¹ſum ¹³donum ²Deus.
Eccleſ 5 19.

8 Qui ¹ſum ¹¹homo ex omnis ³ſuus labor,
& ex afflictio ³ſuus ²animus ¹⁹qui ille ¹laboro
ſub ſol? *Eccleſ* 2 22

9 Quemadmodum ⁷prodeo ex uterus ³ſuus
²mater, ³nudus ¹reverto ²⁴abeo ut ⁷venio, &
¹⁰reporto ⁶nihil ex ³ſuus labor ⁶qui ⁷defero in
³ſuus manus *Eccleſ* 5 15

10. ³Hc ¹²ſum ³magnus ¹³malum, quod
omnino prout ⁷venio ita ⁷abeo ,& ³quis emolumentum ¹ſum ¹¹is qui ⁹laboro ²¹ventus? *Ec* 5 16.

𝕷𝖆𝖓𝖉.

1 Qui ⁹colo ³ſuus ⁶tellus, ⁷habeo ⁶copia
²panis, vero qui ⁹ſector ³vanus ⁶homo, ⁷ſatior
⁶paupertas 28 19

2 Ne ⁵moveo ²antiquus ⁶terminus ⁶+³qui
³tuus majores ¹pono 22 28

3. Propter defectio ²Regio ¹⁴multus ¹ſum
princeps ²is, autem ab homo ³prudens &³peri-
tus ſtatus ²ille ¹prorogor 23 2

𝕷𝖆𝖚𝖌𝖍𝖙𝖊𝖗.

1 Etiam inter riſus animus ¹doleo, & finis
ille ²lætitia ¹ſum ¹ˈmœror 14 13

2. Ego ¹dico de riſus, ¹ſum ¹⁴inſanus, & de
lætitia ⁶ecquis facio ³iſte? *Eccl.ſ* 2. 2

D 2   3. Luctus

3 Sorrow is better than *laughter*, for by the sadnefs of the countenance the heart is made better *Ecclef.* 7 3

4 There is a time to weep, and a time to laugh, a time to mourn, and a time to dance *Ecclef* 3 4

5 As the crackling of thorns under a pot, fo is the *laughter* of the fool *Ecclef* 7 6

Law.

1 The *law* of the wife is a fountain of life, to depart from the fnares of death 13 14

2 Where there is no vifion, the people perifh, but he that keepeth the *law*, happy is he 29 18

3 They that forfake the *law*, praife the wicked, but fuch as keep the *law*, contend with them 28 4

Liberal.

1 The liberal foul fhall be made fat, and he that watereth, fhall be watered alfo himfelf 11 25

Lips.

1 The *lips* of the righteous feed many, but fools die for want of wifdom 10. 21

2 The *lips* of the righteous know what is acceptable, but the mouth of the wicked fpeaketh frowardnefs. 10. 32

3 The *lips* of the wife difperfe knowledge, but the heart of the foolifh doth not fo 15 7

4 In the *lips* of him that hath underftanding, wifdom is found but a rod is for the back of him that is void of underftanding 10 13

5 The words of a wife man's mouth are gracious but the *lips* of a fool will fwallow up himfelf *Eccl.* 10 12.

6 Burning *lips* and a wicked heart, are like a potfherd covered with filver drofs 26 23

Lot.

1 The *lot* is caft into the lap, but the whole difpofing thereof is of the Lord. 16 33

2 The

3 Luctus ¹ fum ¹⁴ melior ¹⁵ rifus, quia ²⁹ tri-
ftitia ² vultus ¹ efficior animus ¹⁴ melior. *Eccl* 7. 3.

4 ¹ Sum tempus ⁵² fleo, & ²⁻ tempus ⁵⁻ rideo,
tempus ⁵² plango, & ²² tempus ⁵⁻ falto. *Ecc* 3 4

5 Ut crepitus ² fpina fub olla, ita ¹ fum rifus
- ftolidus *Ecclef* 7 6

Law.

1 Doctrina ² fapiens ¹fum ¹ fcaturigo ² vita,
ad -º recedo à tendicula ² mors. 13 14

2 Quum non ¹ fum vifio, populus ¹ pereo, autem qui ⁹ obfervo ⁶ lex, ¹⁺ beatus ¹ fum ille 29. 18.

3 Qui ⁹ derelinquo ⁶ lex, ⁷ laudo ⁶ impio-
bus, & qui ⁹ obfervo ⁶ lex, ⁷ contendo cum ille.
28 4

Liberal.

1 ³ Beneficus animus ¹ efficior ¹⁴ pinguis, &
qui ⁵ rigo, ⁷ rigor etiam ipfe 11 25

Lips.

1 Labium ² juftus ¹ pafco ⁶ multus, vero ftultus
⁻ morior præ dementia 10 21

2 Labium ¡ juftus ¹ experior quis ¹ fum ¹⁴ gratus, vero os ² improbus ¹ loquor ⁶ perverfitas.
10 32

3 Labium ² fapiens ¹ fpargo ⁶ fcientia, autem
animus ² ftolidus non ¹ facio ita 15 7

4 ¹⁻ Labium ² prudens fapientia ¹ adfum, at
virga ¹ fum ⁴⁵ tergum ² demens 10 13.

5 Verbum ² fapiens ² os ¹ fum ¹⁴ gratiofus,
vero labium ² ftolidus ¹ abforbeo ⁶ fui *Ecc* 10 12

6 ⁻ Ardens labium, & ³ impius ²⁵ cor -º fum
¹⁴ fimilis ²² tefta ⁻ obductus argenteus ¹ fcoria
26. 23

Lot.

1 Sors ¹ conjicior in gremium, autem ³ totus
ratio ² is ¹ fum à Jehova 16 33

2 The *lot* causeth contention to cease, and parteth between the mighty 18 18.

Lye.

1 A wicked doer giveth heed to false lips, a *lyer* giveth ear to a naughty tongue 17 4

2 A *lying* tongue hateth those that are afflicted by it, and a flattering mouth worketh ruin. 26 28

3 A proud look, a *lying* tongue and hands that shed innocent blood, the Lord hates 6 17.

4 A false witness shall not be unpunished, and he that speaketh lies shall not escape 19 5

5 The lip of truth shall be established for ever, but a *lying* tongue is but for a moment 12 19

6 A righteous man hateth *lying*, but a wicked man is loathsome, and cometh to shame 13 5

7 *Lying* lips are an abomination unto the Lord, but they that deal truly are his delight 12 32.

8 The getting of treasures by a *lying* tongue, is a vanity tossed to and fro of them that seek death 21 6

9 Remove far from me vanity and *lies* give me neither poverty nor riches, feed me with food convenient for me 30 8

Mercy.

1. Mercy and truth preserve the king, and his throne is upholden by *mercy*. 20 28

2 The *merciful* man doeth good to his own soul, but he that is cruel troubleth his own flesh 11 17

3. He that despiseth his neighbour, sinneth, but he that hath *mercy* on the poor, happy is he 14 21

Messenger

1 A wicked *messenger* falleth into mischief, but a faithful ambassadour is health 13. 17

2 As

2. Sors ¹ facio ⁶ contentio ²⁴ cess⁽, & ¹⁰ dii-
mo inter robust ı, ı8 ı8

Lye.

1 Malefi_us ¹ attendo ad f_sus labium, & mendax ¹ adverto ⁶ auris ad ² ærumnosus lingua 17 4

2 Mendax lingua ¹ odi ⁶⁺³ ille qui vatteror
³ille, & ² bardus es ¹ efficio ⁶ ruina ₂6 -8

3 Elatus ⁶ oculus, ² mendax ⁹ lingua ¹ ma-
nusq, effundens ² innocens ²¹ fangu s, ¹ Jehova
¹ odi 6 ı7

4 ³ Fallus testis non ¹ sum ¹⁴ impunis, & q ı
⁹ loquor ⁶ mendacium non ⁷ evado 19 5

5 Labium ² verax ¹ stabilior in æternum autem
² mendax lingua ¹ duro tantum ad momentum.
ı₂ ı9

6 Justus ¹ odi ⁶ mendacium, vero improbus
¹ sum ¹⁴ fœtidus, & ¹⁰ pervenio ad prubrium ı3 5

7 ³ Mendax labium ¹ sum ¹² abominatio 45 Jehova, autem qui ⁹ ago fideliter ⁷ sum ² is ¹³ delec-
tatio ı2 3₂

8 Acquisitio ² thesau us per ³ mendax lingua,
¹ sum ¹² vanitas ² impulsus hu- & illuc à quærens
¹ mors 2 6

9. ⁵ Amo veo longe à ego ⁶ vanitas & ²³ mendacium, ⁵ do ⁴⁵ ego nec ⁶ paupertas, nec ²⁵ divitiæ,
⁵ alu ⁶ ego ²⁹ cibus commodus ²² ego ₃₀ 8.

Mercy.

1 Benignitas & ²³ fides ³⁰ custodio ⁶ rex, & ²⁷il-
le solium ¹ sustentor ²⁹ ben gnitas. 20 28

2 ² Benignus vir ¹ benefacio ² suus ¹² a ı¹m²
autem ² crudelis ¹ in bo- suus ⁶ caro. ıı ı7

3. Qu ⁹ contemno ³ suus ⁶ proximus ⁷ pecco,
autem qui ⁹ facio ⁶ grat a ²⁵ pauper, ¹⁴ beatus ¹ sum
ille ı4 2ı **Messenger**

1 ³ Improbus nuntius ¹ incido in malum, at
² fidelis legatus sum ¹² salus ı3 ı7.

2. Ut

2 As the cold of snow in the time of harvest, so is a faithful *messenger* to them that send him, for he refresheth the soul of his masters 25 13

3 An evil man seeketh only rebellion, therefore a cruel *messenger* shall be sent against him 7 11

Money.

1 A feast is made for laughter, and wine maketh merry, but *money* answereth all things *Eccles* 10 19

Morrow.

1 Boast not thy self of to *morrow*, for thou knowest not what a day may bring forth 27 1

Mouth.

1 A man shall eat good by the fruit of his *mouth*, but the soul of the transgressors shall eat violence 13 2

2. A man shall be satisfied with good by the fruit of his *mouth*, and the recompence of a man's hands shall be rendred unto him 12 14

3 A man's belly shall be satisfied with the fruits of his *mouth*, and with the encrease of his lips shall he be filled 18 20

4 He that keepeth his *mouth*, keepeth his life, but he that openeth wide his lips, shall have destruction 13 3

5 By the blessing of the upright, the city is exalted, but is overthrown by the *mouth* of the wicked 11 11

6 The words of the wicked are to lie in wait for blood, but the *mouth* of the upright shall deliver them 12 6

7. Thou art snared with the words of thy *mouth*, thou art taken with the words of thy *mouth* 6 2

8 A fool's *mouth* is his destruction, and his lips are the snare of his soul. 18. 7

9. Suffer

2 Ut frigus nivalis tempus messis, ita sum fidelis legatus mittens ipse, nam restituo anima suus dominus 5

3 Malus quæro tantum rebellio, idcirco crudelis nuntius mittor in is 17 11.

Money.

1 Convivium peroro ad lætitia, & vinum lætifico, at pecunia sufficio omnis res Ecclf 10. 19

Morrow.

1 Glorior ne de dies crastinus, quia nescio quis dies pario 27 1

Mouth.

1 Vir comedo bonum ex fructus suus or, vero anima perfidiofus comedo violentia 13

2 Vir satior bonum ex fructus suus os, & retributio suus manus re ? or 12

3 Homo venter satior fructus suus os, & proventus suus labium satior ipse 18

4 Qui custodio suus os, conservo suus vita, fed qui divarico suus labium, invenio contritio 13 3

5 Bene ? rectus urbs efferor, aut n destruo os improbus 11 11

6 Verbum improbus infidior sanguis, autem os rectus eripio ille 12 6

7 Illaqueor sermo tuus os, capior sermo tuus os 6

3 Stolidus os sum is contritio & is labium sum tendicula ille vita 18 7

D 5   9

9 Suffer not thy *mouth* to cause thy flesh to ſi , neither ſay thou before the angel it was an error, wherefore ſhould God be angry at thy voice, and deſtroy the works of thy hands ? *Ec-clef* 5 6

Name.

1. A good *name* is rather to be choſen than great riches, and a loving favour rather than ſil-ver and gold 22 1

2 A good *name* is better than precious oint-ment and the day of death than the day of one's birth *Ecclef* 7 1

3 The *name* of the Lord is a ſtrong tower, the righteous runneth into t and is ſafe 18 10.

Naught.

1. It is *naught*, it is *naught*, ſaith the buyer, but when he is gone his way, then he boaſteth 20 14.

Neighbour.

1 He that is void of wiſdom, deſpiſeth his *neighbour*, but a man of underſtanding holdeth his peace 11 12

2 Say not unto thy *neighbour*, go and come again, and to morrow I will give, when thou haſt it by thee 3 28

3 A man that flattereth his *neighbour*, ſpread-eth a net for his feet 29 5

4 As a madman who caſteth firebrands, ar-rows and death, ſo is the man that deceiveth his *neighbour* and ſaith, am not I in ſport ? 26 18, 9

Net

1 In vain the *net* is ſpread in the ſight of any bird 1 17

News.

1 As cold water is to a thirſty ſoul, ſo is good *news* from a far country 25 25.

Oppreſſion,

y Ne> Permitto ut 3 tuus os 1 facio 3 tuus (caro 24 pecco neque 5 dico coram angelus, 2 ille 1 fum error, quare Deus 1 fuccenfeo p oprer tuus vox, & 0 perdo 6 opus 3 tuus 2 manus Ecclef 5 6.

Name.

1. 2 Bonus fama 1 fum 14 optatior 3 amplus 15 divitiæ, & 20 gratia 3 melior 15 argentum & 20 aurum 22 1

2. 2 bonus fama 1 fum 14 melior 5 pretiofus 15 unguentum, & 23 dies 2 mors 15 dies 2 nativitas Ecl f 7. 1

3 Nomen 2 Jehova 1 fum 5 robuftus turris juftus 1 accurro ad 2 ille & 10 fum 14 falvus Id 10

Naught.

1. 1 Sum peffimu, 1 fum peffimu, 1 aio emptor, fed quum 7 digredior, tum 7 glorior 20 14

Neighbour.

1 Qui 9 careo 6 fapientia. fperno fuus 6 proximus, at vir prudens 1 fileo 11. 12

2 5 Dico ne 2 tuus 16 proximes, 5 abeo de re 1 reverto, & cras 5 do, quum 1 fum ille penes tu 3 28.

3 Vir qui 9 blandior 2 fuus 2 proximat, 2 pando 6 rete contra 2 is pes 29 5

4 Ut infaniens qui 9 jaculor 2 fax, 6 fagitta & 2 lethale, ita 1 fum ille qui 9 decipio ille 6 proximus, & 9 dico, nonne 2 ludo 26 18, 9.

Net.

1 Fruftra rete 1 pando ante oculus 2 aves 1. 17

News.

1 Ut frigidus aqua teffus 45 animu, ita 1 fum 2 bonus auditio e longinquus terra 25 25.

Dpp efRod.

Oppression

1 He that oppresseth the poor, reproacheth his maker, but he that honoureth him, hath mercy on the poor 14 31

2 A poor man that oppresseth the poor is like a sweeping rain which leaveth no food 28 3

3 Oppression maketh a wise man mad, and a gift destroyeth the heart Eccls 7 7

4 The prince that wanteth understanding is also a great oppressor, but he that hateth covetousness shall prolong his days 28 16

5. I considered all the oppressions that are done under the sun, and beheld the tears of such as were oppressed, and they had no comforter, and on the side of their oppressors, there was power, but they had no comforter Eccls 4 1

6 If thou see the oppression of the poor and violent perverting of judgment and justice in a province, marvel not at the matter, for he that is higher than the highest regardeth it, and there be higher than they Eccls 5 8

Ox.

1 Where no oxen are, the crib is clean, but much increase is by the strength of the ox 14 4

Pit.

1 Whoso diggeth a pit, shall fall therein, and he that rolleth a stone it shall return upon him 26 27

2 Whoso causeth the righteous to go astray in an evil way, he shall fall himself into his own pit, but the upright shall have good things in possession 28 10

3 He that diggeth a pit, shall fall into it, and whoso breaketh a hedge, a serpent shall bite him, Eccls 10 8

Oppreſſion.

1 Qui opprim⁹ ⁶ reⁱaⁱs, ⁵ probum ⁷afficio - ıs ⁶ Crea⁻or, autem quı ⁹ honoro ⁶₊³ hıc, ⁷ facio gratıa -⁵ egens 14 31

2 Pauper quı ⁹ opprımo ⁰ pauper ¹ ſum ³ ſimılıs ³ everrens ²⁻ pluvıa ³ quı ⁹ relınquo ³ nullus ⁶ panıs 28 23

3 Oppreſſıo ¹ facio ⁶ ſapıens ınfaⁿus, & doⁱum ¹ perdo ⁶ anımus. *Ecclef* 7 7

4 Prınceps ³ quı 9 careo ⁸ ıntellıgentıa ¹ ſum etıam ³ durus ⁱ⁰ oppreſⁱr, autem quı ⁹ oⁱı ⁶ quæſtus⁻ prolongo ² ıs ⁶ dıeⁱ 8 16

5 ⁵ Conſıdero ³ omnıs ⁶ oppreſſıo ³ quı ⁹ fıo ſub ſol, & ¹⁰ reſpıcıo ⁶ lacryma ² ıs quı ⁹ opprımor & ¹ ſum ¹¹ ılle ³ nullus conſolⁱⁿor, & penes opprımⁱⁱs ¹ ſum vⁱres, ſⁱd ¹¹ ıs ¹ ſum ³ nullus conſolatoⁱ *Eccl ſ* 4 1

6 ⁵ Sı vıdeo ⁶ oppreſſıo ² pauper & ³ vıolentus ınveⁱıo - juⁱ & ⁻⁻ juⁱtıⁱıa ın provıncıa, ³ mıror ne ³ ne de ⁵ ılle ınſtıtutum, nam quı ⁹ ſum ¹⁴ altıor ¹⁵ altıſſımus ⁷ obſervo, & ⁷ ſum ¹⁴ ſuperıor ¹⁵ ılle *Eccleſ* 5 8

Ox.

1 Ubı non ¹ ſum bos, præcepe ¹ ſum ³ mundus autem ⁵ multus proventus ı ſum ²⁹ vıres bos 14 4

Pit.

1 Quı ⁹ fodıo ⁵ fovea, decıdo ın ³ ıs, & quı ⁹ devolvo ⁶ lapıs ¹ reverto ın ıpſe 26 27

2 Quı ⁹ facio ⁶ ıectus ²⁴ vagor ın ³ malus vıa ¹ decıdo ıpſe ın ³ ſuus fovea, vero ınteger ¹ poſſıdeo ⁶ bonum 28 1⁰.

3 Quı ⁹ fodıo ⁶ foſſa ⁷ cado ın ³ ıs, & quı ⁵ perrumpo ⁶ ſepes, ſerpens ¹ mordeo ⁶₊³ ıs *Ecclef* 1⁰ 8

Poor

1 He that loveth pleasure shall be a *poor* man, he that loveth wine and oil shall not be rich 21 17

2 Be not among wine-bibbers, among riotous eaters of flesh, for the drunkard and the glutton shall come to poverty, and drowsiness shall cloath a man with rags 23 20 21

3 Love not sleep, lest thou come to poverty, open thine eyes, and thou shalt be satisfied with bread 20 13

4 Yet a little sleep a little slumber a little folding of the hands to sleep, so shall thy poverty come as one that travelleth, and thy want as an armed man. 24 33 34

5 He that hasteth to be rich hath an evil eye, and considereth not that poverty shall come upon him 28 22

6 The ransom of a man's life are his riches but the *poor* heareth not rebuke 13 8.

7 There is that maketh himself rich yet hath nothing, there is that maketh himself *poor*, yet hath great riches

8 The desire of a man is his kindness, and a *poor* man is better than a liar 20 22

9 Better is the *poor* that walketh in his uprightness, than he that is perverse in his ways, though he be rich 28 6

10 Wealth maketh many friends, but the *poor* is separated from his neighbour 19 4

11 All the brethren of the *poor* do hate him; how much more do his friends go far from him he pursueth them with words, yet they are wanting to him 19 7

12 The *poor* is hated even of his own neighbour, but the rich hath many friends 14 20

13 The

Prov.

1 Qui 9 amo 9 voluptas 7 sum 3 egens 1, vir, qui 9 amo 6 vinum & 2, unguentum non 1 sum 1 dives, 21 17

2 1,5 Versor ne inter vinosus, inter vorator 2 caro, nam ebrius & 2, comessator 3,0 pervenio ad paupertas, & dormitatio 1 induo 6 homo 5, pann culus 23 20, 21

3 5 Diligo ne 6 somnus, ne 5 pervenio ad paupertas, 5 aperio 3 tuus 6 oculus, & 1 satior 8 panis. 20 13

4 Adhuc 3 pauculus somnus 3 pauculus dormitatio, 3 pauculus complicatio 2 manus ad 4 dormito, ita 3 tuus paupertas 1 advenio ut viator, & 3 tuus 2 egestas tanquam 3 clypeatus vir 24 33, 34

5 Qui 9 accelero ad 20 ditesco, 1 habeo 3 malignus 6 oculus & 10 ignoro 54 1 opia 24 advenio 1 ille 28 22

6 Redemptio 2 vir 2 vita 1 sum 3 suus 13 divitiae at paupe 1 audio non 6 increpatio 13. 8.

7 7 Sum qui 9 jacto 6 sui 3 d ves, tamen 7 habeo 6 nihil, 7 sum qui 9 fingo 6 sui pauper, tamen 7 habeo 3 amplus 6 substantia

8 Desiderium 2 homo 1 sum 2 ipse 1, benignitas & pauper 1 sum 14 melior 15 mendax 19 22.

9 14 Melior 1 sum pauper ambulans in 3 suus integritas, 15 + 3 ille qui 9 sum 14 perversus in suus iter, quamvis 1 sum 13 dives. 2, 6

10 Substantia 1 addo 3 multus 6 amicus, autem tenuis 1 disjungor a 3 suus proximus 19 4

11 3 Omnis frater 2 pauper 1 odi 6 ille, quanto magis 2 is socius 1 absum procul ab ille 3 persequor 1 + 3 ille 29 verbum, tamen ille non 1 adsum 17 ille 1,9 7

12 Pauper 1 sum 3 exosus etiam 3 suus 55 proximus, sed 11 dives 1 sum multus amicus 14 10.

13 Dives

13 The rich ruleth over the *poor*, and the borrower is servant to the lender 22 7

14 The *poor* useth intreaties, but the rich answereth roughly 18 23

15 There is a generation whose teeth are as swords, and their jaw-teeth as knives, to devour the *poor* from the earth, and the needy from among men 30 14

16 Rob not the *poor* because he is *poor*, neither oppress the afflicted in the gate 22 22

17 He that oppresseth the *poor* to increase his riches, and he that giveth to the rich, shall surely come to want 22. 16

18 Whoso mocketh the *poor*, reproacheth his maker, and he that is glad at calamities, shall not be unpunished 17 5

19 The rich and *poor* meet together, the Lord is the maker of them all 22. 2.

20 He that hath pity upon the *poor* lendeth unto the Lord, and that which he hath given, will he pay him again 18 17

21 The righteous considereth the cause of the poor, but the wicked regardeth not to know it 29 27

22 Whoso stoppeth his ears at the cry of the poor, he shall also cry himself but shall not be heard 21 13 !

23 Open thy mouth, judge righteously, and plead the cause of the *poor* and needy 31 9

Portion.

1 Give a *portion* to seven and also to eight, for thou knowest not what evil shall be upon the earth *Ecclef* 11. 2.

Praise.

1 As the fining pot for silver and the furnace for gold so is a man to his *praise* 27 21.

2 Let

13 Dives ¹ dominor in pauper & mutuans ¹ ſum ¹⁹ ſervus ⁴⁾ commodans 22 7

14 Pauper ¹ eloquor ⁶ ſupplicatio, autem dives ¹ loquor aſpere 18 23

15 ¹ Sum generatio 9 qui dens ¹ ſum ut ²⁵ gladius & ² is ⁴⁾ molaris ut ² culter, ad ²⁰ conſumo ⸱ pauper è terra & ²³ egens ab homo 30 14

16 ⁵ Spolio ne ⁶ tenuis eo quod ¹ ſum ¹⁴ tenuis, neque ⁵ contero ⁶ pauper in porta 22 22

17 Qui 9 opprimo ⁶ tenuis ut ⁷ amplifico ⁹ ſuus ⁶ res, & qui 9 do ²⁵ dives, certe ⁷ devenio ad egeſtas 22 16

18 Qui 9 ſubſanno ¹⁷ pauper, ⁷ convitior ² is ⁶ Creator, & qui 9 delector 4ᴸ calamitas, non ⁷ ſum ¹⁴ impunis 17 5

19 Dives & ²³ pauper ³⁰ occurro unaˊ Jehova ¹ ſum ¹³ Creator ²+ ³ hic ²⁴ ³ omnis. 22. 2

20 Qui 9 largior 25 pauper, ⁷ mutuo ²¹ Jehova, & 9 qui ⁷ do, ille ¹ rependo ²⁵ ipſe 19 7.

21 Juſtus ¹ cognoſco ⁶ cauſa ² tenuis, at improbus ¹ animadverto non ut ⁷ cognoſco ⁶+⁹ ille 29 7.

22 Qui 9 obturo ³ ſuus ⁶ auris à clamor ² tenuis, ille etiam ¹ clamo ipſe, at non ⁷ exaudior. 21 13

⸱ 23 ⁵ Aperio ³ tuus ⁶ os, ⁵ judico juſte & ¹⁰ ago ¹ cauſa ² pauper & ²⁵ egens 31 9

Portion.

1 ⁵ Do ⁶ pars ²⁵ ſeptem aut etiam ²⁵ octo, nam neſcio ⁹ quis malum ¹ ſum ⁹ futurus ſuper terra *Eccleſ* 11 2.

Praiſe.

1 Sicut ³ fuſorius vas 45 argentum & ²³ catinus 45 aurum, ita ¹ ſum vir ⁹ ſuus 45 laus ²⁷ 21.

2 Alius

2. Let another man *praise* thee, and not thy own mouth a stranger, and not thy own lips 27 2

Pride.

1 Only by *pride* cometh contention, but with the well advised is wisdom 3 10

2 When *pride* cometh, then cometh shame, but with the lowly is wisdom 11 2

3 An high look and a *proud* heart, and the plowing of the wicked is sin 21 4

4 Every one that is *proud* in heart, is an abomination to the Lord, though hand join in hand, he shall not be unpunished 16 5

5 He that is of a *proud* heart, stirreth up strife, but he that putteth his trust in the Lord, shall be made fat. 28. 25

6 Better is the end of a thing than the beginning thereof and the patient in spirit is better than the *proud* in spirit *Eccles* 7 8

7 *Proud* and haughty scorner is his name, who dealeth in *proud* wrath 21 24.

Prudent.

1 A *prudent* man concealeth knowledge, but the heart of fools proclaimeth foolishness 12 23

2 The wisdom of the *prudent* is to understand his way, but the folly of fools is deceit 14 8

3 The wise in heart shall be called *prudent*, and the sweetness of the lips encreaseth learning 16 21

4 A *prudent* man foreseeth the evil, and hideth himself, but the simple pass on and are punished 22 3.

5 The simple believeth every word but the *prudent* man looketh well to his going 14 15

Prince.

1 Delight is not seemly for a fool, much less for a servant to have rule over *princes*. 19 10

2. Many

2 Alius [1] laudo [6] tu, autem non [2] tuus os , extraneus, autem non [3] tuus labium 27 2.

Pride.

1 [2] Solus [29] superbia [1] prodeo jurgium, at penes consultus [1] sum sapientia. 13 10

2 Cum superbia [1] advenio, tum [1] accedo ignominia, autem apud modestus [1] sum sapientia 11.2.

3 [2] Elatus oculus, & [3] superbus [2] cor, & [2] aratio [2] improbus [30] sum [1] peccatum 21 24

4 Omnis [3] altus [37] animus [1] sum [13] ab minatio [1] Jhova, licet manus [1] co jungor ad manus, non [7] sum [14] impunitus. 16 5.

5 Qui [9] sum [2] superbus [18] animus [2] misceo [6] contentio, autem qui [9] confido [4] Jehova, [2] efficior [14] pinguis 28. 25

6 [14] Melior [1] sum finis [2] res [15] principium - is, & longanimus [1] sum [14] melior quam [2] elatus animus *Ecclef* 7 8

7 Superbus & [2] contumax, derisor [1] sum [2] ipse [13] nomen, qui [9] ago cum [2] superbus excandescentia 21. 24

Prudent.

1 [2] Callidus homo [1] tego [6] scientia, autem animus [2] stolidus [1] proclamo [6] stultitia 2 23

2 Sapientia - astutus [1] sum [24] considero [2] suus [1] via, sed stultitia [2] stolidus [1] sum [13] do us 14 8.

3 Sapiens [3] animus [1] vocor [14] prudens, autem suavitas [2] labium [1] addo [6] scientia 16 21

4 Astutus [1] praevideo [6] malum, & [10] abscondo [5] su , autem fatuus [1] transeo & [10] mulcto 22 3

5 Fatuus [1] credo [3] omnis [4] verbum, autem astutus [1] adverto ad [2] suus gressus 14 15

Prince.

1 Oblectatio non decet [2] stultus, mul o minus [6] e vus [24] dominor in princeps 19 10

2 Multus

2 Many will intreat the favour of the *prince*, and every man is a friend to him that giveth gifts 19 6

3 By long forbearing is a *prince* perfuaded, and a foft tongue breaketh the bone 25 5

Proclaim.

1 Moft men will *proclaim* every one his own goodnefs, but a faithful man who can find 20 6

Quiet

1 Whofo herrkens to me (wifdom) fhall dwell fafely and fhall be *quiet* from fear of evil 1 33

2 Better is a dry *morfel* and *quietnefs* therewith, than a houfe full of facrifices with ftrife 17 1

3 Better is a handful with quietnefs than both the hands full, with travail and affliction therewith. *Ecclef* 4 6

Rebuke.

1 Open *rebuke* is better than fecret love 27 5

2. A wife fon heareth his father's inftruction, but a fcorner heareth not *rebuke* 13 1

3 To them that *rebuke* him (the wicked) fhall be delight and a good bleffing fhall come upon them 24 25

4 He that *reproveth* a fcorner getteth to himfelf fhame, and he that *rebuketh* a wicked man getteth himfelf a blot 9 7

5 He that *rebuketh* a man, fhall afterwards find more favour, than he that flattereth with the tongue 28 23

Recompence.

1 Say not thou, I will *recompence* evil, but wait on the the Lord, and he fhall fave thee 20 22

Reproved.

. Multus [1] precor [6] favor [2] Princeps, & quifque [1] fum [12] amicus [45] ille qui [9] do [6] munus.
19 6

[3] , Longanimitas Princeps [1] exoror, & [3] mol-
li lingua frango [6] os 25 15.

Proclaim.

[1] Plurimus homo [1] prædico quifque [3] fuus
[2] bonitas, aurem [3] verax [6] vir quis [1] invenio.
[?] o 6.

Quiet.

Quicunque [1] aufculto [41] ego (fapientia) [7] habito fecure, & [10] fum [14] tranquillus a pavor
malum 1. 33

- . Melior [1] fum ficcus buccea & tranquillitas cum is, quam [3] domus [3] plenus [40] facri-
ficium cum contentio 17 1

, [11] Melior [1] fum vola [3] plenus cum quies,
quam ambo [20] manus [3] plenus cum moleftia &
afflictio [2] fpiritus *Ecclef* 4 6

Rebuke.

[1] . Manifeftus correptio [1] fum [11] melior [3] occultus [13] amor 27 5

[2] Sapiens filius [1] aufculto [3] fuus [2] pater [?] erudio, at derifor [1] aufculto non [6] increpatio
13 1

[3]. [12] Ille qui [9] corripio [6+3] is (improbus)
[3] fum amœnitas, & [3] bonus benedictio [1] obvenio
15 [?]4 25

[4] Qui [9] erudio [6] derifor, [7] recipio [21] fui [6] ignominia, & qui [9] corripio [6] improbus [7] recipio
fui [6] convitium 9 7

[5] Qui [9] corripio [6] homo poftea [7] confequor
major [6] gratia, quam qui [9] blandior [3] lingua
.8 23.

Recompence.

[1] Ne [5] dico, [5] rependo [6] malum, autem [5] ex-
pecto [5] Jehova, & [7] fervo [6] tu. 20 22

Reprover.

Reprover.

1. As an ear-ring of gold, and an ornament of fine gold, so is a wise reprover unto an obedient ear

2 The ear that heareth the reproof of life, abideth among the wise. 15 31

3 Smite a scorner, and the simple will beware, and reprove one that hath understanding, and he will understand knowledge 19. 25

4 He that being often reproved hardeneth his neck, shall suddenly be destroyed, and that without remedy 29 1

Respect.

1 It is not good to have respect of persons in judgment 24 23

2 To have respect of persons, is not good, for, for a piece of bread that man will transgress. 28. 21

Rich.

1 Labour not to be rich, cease from thy own understanding 23 4

2 Riches profit not in the day of wrath, but righteousness delivereth from death 11 4.

3. Wilt thou set thine eyes upon that which is not? for riches certainly make themselves wings, they away as an eagle towards heaven 23 5

4 Riches are not for ever, and doth the crown endure to every generation? 27 14

5 The sleep of a labouring man is sweet, whether he eat little or much, but the abundance of the rich will not suffer him to sleep Eccles 5 12

6 A faithful man shall abound with blessings, but he that maketh haste to be rich, shall not be innocent. 28 20

7 He that trusteth in his riches shall fall, but the righteous shall flourish as a branch. 11. 28.

8 The

Repʒover.

1 Velut monile ³ aureus & ²³ ornamentum ex
inſignis aurum, ita ſum ² ſapiens reprehenſor
¹ auſcultans ⁴ auris

2 Auris ² auſcultans ³¹ correptio ² vita, ¹ commoror inter ſapiens 15 31

3 ⁵ Percutio ⁶ deriſor, & fatuus ¹ caveo, &
¹ corripio ⁶+ qui ⁹ poſſideo ⁶ prudentia, & ⁷ intelligo ⁵ ſcientia 16 25

4 Vir qui ſæpius ² correptus, ¹ obduro ³ ſuus
⁵ cervix, repente ⁷ perdo, idque ſine curatio
19 ¹

Reſpect.

1 Non ¹² ſum ¹¹ bonus, agnoſco ⁶ perſona in
judicium 24 23

2 Agnoſco ⁶ perſona, non ¹² ſum ¹⁴ bonus,
nim propter buccea ² panis ³ ille vir ¹ deficio.
28 21

Rich.

1 ⁵ Laboro ne ut ⁵ diteſco, ⁵ deſiſto à ⁷ tuus
prudentia 23 4.

2 Divitiæ non ¹ proſum ⁴ dies ² furor, autem juſtitia ¹ eripio à mors 11. 4

3 An ⁵ figo ⁶ oculus in ille qui non ⁹ ſum ²
enim opes certe ¹ comparo ²¹ ſui ⁶ ala, ¹ avolo
ut ²⁵ aquila verſus cœlum. 23 5

4 Divitiæ ¹ ſum non in ſeculum; & an corona ¹ maneo in ⁵ quiſque generatio 27 24

5 Somnus ² laborans ¹ ſum ¹⁴ dulcis, ſive
⁵ comedo parum ſive multum, autem ſaturitas
⁵ dives non ¹ permitto ⁶+³ is ut ⁷ dormio *Ec.*5 12.

6 ⁵ Fidelis vir ¹ abundo ⁸ benedictio, at qui
⁵ præcipito ad ²⁰ diteſco non ⁷ ſum ¹⁴ innocens.
28 20.

7 Qui ⁹ confido ³ ſuus ⁴³ divitiæ ⁷ decido, at
juſtus ¹ effloreſco tanquam ²³ ramus. 11. 28.

8. ² **Dives**

8 The rich man's wealth is his strong city, and as an high wall in his own conceit 18 11

9. There is a sore evil that I have seen under the sun, namely, *riches* kept for the owners thereof to their hurt but those *riches* perish by evil travail, and he begetteth a son, and there is nothing in his hand *Eccles.* 5. 13, 14

10 A man to whom God hath given riches, wealth and honour, so that he wanteth nothing for his soul of all that he desireth, yet God giveth him not power to eat thereof, but a stranger eateth it, this is vanity, and it is an evil disease. *Eccles* 6 2

11 By knowledge shall the chambers be filled with all precious and pleasant *riches* 24

Righteous.

1 The *righteous* is more excellent than his neighbour but the way of the wicked seduceth them. 12. 26

2 The mouth of a *righteous* man is a well of life, but violence covereth the mouth of the wicked 10 11

3 He (the slothful) coveteth all day long, but the *righteous* giveth and spareth not 21 26

4 When the *righteous* are in authority, the people rejoice, but when the wicked beareth rule, the people mourn 29 2

5 In the transgression of an evil man there is a snare, but the *righteous* doth sing and rejoice 29 6

6 When *righteous* men do rejoice, there is great glory, but when the wicked rise, a man is hidden 28 12

7 When it goeth well with the *righteous*, the city rejoiceth, and when the wicked perish, there is shouting 11 10

8 [2]Dives substantia [1]sum [2]is [3]munitus urbs, & tanquam [3]altus [23]murus in [2]ipse cogitatio 18. 11.

9 [1]Sum [5]magnus malum [6+3]qui [5]videor sub sol, scilicet divitiæ [3]asservatus [31]dominus [2+]is in [2]ipse malum, at [3]ille divitiæ [1]pereo [3]malus [9]occupatio, & [7]gigno [6]filius, & [1]sum nihil in [2]is manus *Ecclef* 5 13, 14

10. Vir [25]qui Deus [1]do [6]divitiæ, [6]facultas & [3]honor, adeo ut [7]indigeo [3]nullus [8]res pro suus anima ex omnis [6+3]qui [7]concupisco, tamen Deus [1]facio [25]is [6]non copia [52]comedo ex ille, sed alienus [1]comedo [6+]ille, [3]hic [1]sum vanitas & [14]sum [3]malus ægritudo. *Ecclef.* 6. 2.

11 [29]Scientia penetrale [1]impleor [3]omnis pretiosus & [3]amœnus [8]opes 24 4.

Righteous.

1 Justus [1]sum [14]excellentior [5]suus [14]proximus, at via [2]improbus [1]seduco [6+]is 12. [6]

2 Os [2]justus [1]sum [13]scaturigo [2]vita, at violentia [1]obtego [6]os [2]improbus. 10 11.

3 Ille (piger) [1]desidero [3]totus [4]dies, vero justus [1]do neque [10]parco 21 26

4 Cum justus [1]impero, populus [1]lætor, autem cum improbus [1]dominor, populus [1]suspi ro 29 2.

5 [17]Defectio [3]malus [2]vir [1]insum tendicula, autem justus [1]canto & [10]lætor 29. 6

6 Cum justus [1]exulto, [1]sum [3]amplus ornatus, autem quum improbus [1]erigor, homo [1]occultor. 28. 12

7 Cum [27]benefio [17]justus, urbs [1]exulto, & cum improbus [1]pereo, [1]exerceo can'u . 11 10,

8 A righteous man regardeth the life of his beaft, but the tender mercies of the wicked are cruel 12 10

9 He that fpeaketh truth, fheweth forth righteoufnefs, but a falle witnefs, deceit 12 17

10 A righteous man wifely confidereth the houfe of the wicked, but God overthroweth the wicked for their wickednefs 21 12

11 The wicked flee when no man purfueth, but the righteous are bold as a lion. 28 1

12 The way of a flothful man is an hedge of thorns, but the way of the righteous is made plain 15 19

13 The fruit of the righteous is as a tree of life, and he that winneth fouls is wife 11 30

14 The labour of the righteous tendeth to life, the fruit of the wicked to fin 10 16

15 The wicked defireth the net of evil men, but the root of the righteous yieldeth fruit 12 12

16 The fear of the wicked it fhall come upon him, but the defire of the righteous fhall be granted 10. 24

17 The Lord is far from the wicked, but he heareth the prayer of the righteous 15 29

18 The righteous is delivered out of trouble, and the wicked cometh in his ftead 11 8

19 The wicked fhall be a ranfom for the righteous, and the tranfgreffor for the upright 21 18

20 Behold, the righteous fhall be recompenfed in the earth, much more the wicked and the finner. 11 31

21 When the wicked are multiplied, tranfgreffion encreafeth, but the righteous fhall fee their fall 29 16

22 Evil purfueth finners, but to the righteous good fhall be repayed 13 21.

23. The

8 Juſtus ¹ curo ⁶ vita ³ ſuus ² jumentum, autem miſeratio ² improbus ¹ ſum ¹⁴ crudelis 12 10

9 Qui ⁹ loquor ⁶ veritas, ⁷ indico ⁶ juſtitia, autem ³ falſus teſtis, ⁶ dolus. 12 17

10 Juſtus prudenter ¹ conſidero ⁶ domus improbus, at Deus ¹ everto ⁶ improbus propter -ille improbitas. 21 12

11 Improbus ¹ fugio ⁵⁶ nemo perſequens, autem juſtus ¹ ſum ¹⁴ audax tanquam -⁵ leo 28 1

12 Via ² piger ¹ ſum velut ²³ ſepementum ſpina, autem iter ² rectus ¹ fio ¹⁵ planus. 15. 19

13 Fructus ² juſtus ¹ ſum velut ²³ arbor ² vita, & qui ⁹ ſapio ⁶ anima ⁷ ſum ¹⁴ ſapiens 11 30.

14 Labor ² juſtus ¹ tendo in vita, proventus improbus in peccatum. 10 16.

15 Improbus ¹ deſidero ⁶ rete ² malus, ſed radix ² juſtus ¹ do fructus 12 12.

16 Timor ² improbus ¹ evenio ²¹ is, autem deſiderium ² juſtus ¹ concedor. 10 24

17 Jehova ¹¹ abſum procul ab improbus, autem ⁷ exaudio ⁶ oratio ² juſtus 15 29

18 Juſtus ¹ liberor ex anguſt a, & improbus devenio in ² is locus 11 8

19 Improbus ¹ ſum ¹· redemptio pro juſtus, & ²⁵ perfidus pro rectus 21. 18

20 En, juſtus ¹ remuneror in terra, multo magis improbus & - peccator 11 31.

21 Cum improbus multiplicor, defectio ¹ creſco, vero juſtus ¹ video ² is ⁶ caſus 29 16

22 Malum ¹ inſector ⁶ peccator, autem ² juſtus bonum ¹ compenſor 13 2 .

23 Juſtus

23 The *righteous* eateth to the satisfying of his soul, but the belly of the wicked shall want 13 25

24 The Lord will not suffer the soul of the *righteous* to famish, but he casteth away the substance of the wicked 10 3

25. As the whirlwind passeth, so is the wicked no more, but the *righteous* is an everlasting foundation 10 25

26 The *righteous* shall never be removed, but the wicked shall not inhabit the earth 10 30

27 A man shall not be established by wickedness, but the root of the *righteous* shall not be moved. 12 3

28 The light of the *righteous* rejoyceth, but the lamp of the wicked shall be put out 13 9

29 The way of the wicked is an abomination to the Lord; but he loveth him that followeth after *righteousness* 15 9

30 Better is a little with *righteousness*, than great revenues without right 16 8

31 *Righteousness* exalteth a nation, but sin is a reproach to any people. 14 34

32 Treasures of wickedness profit nothing, but *righteousness* delivereth from death 10 2

33 The wicked worketh a deceitful work, but to him that soweth *righteousness* shall be a sure reward 11 18

34. The *righteousness* of the perfect shall direct his way, but the wicked shall fall by his own wickedness 11 5

35 In the way of *righteousness* is life, and in the path-way thereof there is no death. 12 28

36 *Righteousness* keepeth him that is upright in the way, but wickedness overthroweth the sinner. 13. 6.

23. ˙ Juſtus comedo ad ſatietas ³ ſuus ² anima, autem venter ² improbus ¹ egeo. 13 15.

24 Jehova non ¹ ſino ⁶ anima ² juſtus 24 eſurio, autem ⁷ depello ⁶ ſubſtantia ² improbus 10 3.

25 Ut turbo ¹ tranſeo, ita ¹ exiſto improbus non amplius, vero juſtus ¹ ſum ² perpetuus ¹ fundamentum 10 25

16 Juſtus nunquam ¹ dimoveor, vero improbus non ¹ habito ⁶ terra 10 30

17. Homo non ¹ ſtabilior ²⁹ improbitas, autem radix ² juſtus non ¹ dimoveor. 12. 3

28 Lux ² juſtus ¹ lætor ; at lucerna ² improbus ¹ extinguor. 13 9

19 Via ² improbus ¹ ſum ¹⁹ abominatio 45 Jehova, autem ⁷ diligo ⁶＋³ is qui ⁹ ſector ⁶ juſtitia. 15 9

30 ¹⁴ Melior ¹ ſum parvum cum juſtitia, quam ampliſſimus ²³ proventus ſine jus 16 8

31. Juſtitia ¹ exalto ⁶ gens, autem peccatum ſum ¹³ probrum ³ omnis 45 populus 14 34

32 Theſaurus ² improbitas non ¹ proſum, ſed juſtitia ¹ eripio à mors 10 2

33 Improbus ¹ facio ³ fallax ⁶ opus, vero 45 ſerens ³¹ juſtitia ¹ ſum ³ fidus merces 11. 18.

34. Juſtitia ² integer ¹ dirigo ² is ⁶ via, at improbus ¹ cado ³ ſuus ²⁹ improbitas 11 5

35 In iter ² juſtitia ¹ ſum vita, & in ſemita ¹ is ² ſum non mors 12 28.

36 Juſtitia ¹ cuſtodio ⁶ integer in via, vero improbitas ¹ perverto ⁶ peccator 13 6.

37 As *righteousness* tendeth to life, so he that pursueth evil, pursueth it to his own death 11.19

38. Lay not wait, O wicked man, against the dwelling of the *righteous*, spoil not his resting place 24 15.

39 A *righteous* man falling down before the wicked is as a troubled fountain, and corrupt spring. 25 26

40 He that saith unto the wicked, Thou art *righteous*, him shall the people curse, nations shall abhor him 24 24.

41 All things come a like to all, there is one event to the *righteous*, and to the wicked, to the good, to the clean, and to the unclean, to him that sacrificeth, and to him that sacrificeth not. as is the good, so is the sinner, and he that sweareth, as he that feareth an oath *Eccles* 9. 2.

Rule.

1 He that hath no *rule* over his own spirit, is like a city that is broken down, and without walls 25 28

2 There is a time when one man *ruleth* over another to his own hurt 8. 9.

3 As a roaring lion, and a ranging bear, so is a wicked *Ruler* over the poor people 28. 15.

4 If a *Ruler* hearken to lyes, all his servants are wicked 29 12.

5 If the spirit of the *ruler* rise up against thee, leave not thy place, for yielding pacifieth great offences *Eccles* 10 4

6 Be not desirous of his (the *ruler's*) dainties, for they are deceitful meet 23 3

Sacrifice.

1 The *Sacrifice* of the wicked is an abomination to the Lord, but the prayer of the upright is his delight 15 8

2 The

37. Ut juſtitia ˙ tendo ad vita, ſic qui 9 ſector ⁶ malum, ¯ſector ⁶+¯ ille ad ³ ſuus mors ˡˡ 19.

38 Ne ⁵ inſidior, ²⁶ O improbus, ²¹ habitacu-ˡꞵ -juſtus, ⁵ devaſto ne ² ıs ⁶ accubıtus 24 ıς.

39 Juſtus ³ cadens coram improbus ˡ ſum ut contur̊batus ²⁵ fons, & ³ corruptus ²⁵ ſcaturı-⒢ ²⁵ 26

40. Qui 9 dıco ¹⁶ improbus, tu ˡ ſum ¹⁴ juſtus, +⁵ ıs populus ˡ execror, natıo ˡ deteſtor ⁶+³ ıs. 24 24

41 Omnis ˡ evenio æque ²¹ omnis, ˡ ſum ³ i-dem eventus ⁴⁵ juſtus & ²⁵ improbus, & ²³ bo-nus, & ²³ mundus, & immundus, ⁴⁵ ſacrificans, & ³ ıs quı non 9 ſacrifico, ut ˡ ſum bonus, ıta ˡ ſum peccator, & qui 9 juro, ut ille ³ qui 9 re-vereor ⁶ juramentum *Eccleſ.* 9. 2

Rule.

1 Qui 9 habeo ³ nullus ⁶ imperium in ³ ſuus ſpirıtus, ⁷ ſum ¹⁴ ſimilis ²² civitas ³ diſruptus, & abſque murus 25 28

2 ˡ Sum tempus ¹⁹+³ qui homo ˡ dominor ın homo in ³ ſuus malum. 8. 9.

3 Ut ³ rugiens leo & ⁵ diſcurſans ²² urſus, ita ſum impıobus dominator ın ³ tenuis populus. 28 15

4. Sı dominator ˡ attendo ¹⁷ mendacium, ˉom-nis ² ıs minıſter ˡ ſum ¹⁴ improbus 29 12

5 Sı ſpiritus ⁻dom̊ nator ˡ aſcendo contra tu, ˡ deſero ne ³ tuus ⁶ lȯcus. nam ſubmiſſıo ˡ ſedo magnum ⁶ peccatum *Eccleſ* 10 4

6 Ne ⁵ ſum ¹⁺ꜹ dus ²⁵ ıs (² rector) ⁵⁷ cupe dıæ, enim ˡ ſum ꝰ mendax ¹³ cibus 23. 3.

Sacrifice.

1 Sacrificium ⁻improbus ˡ ſum ¹³ abominatio 4 Jehova, atrem oratio ² rectus ˡ ſum ² ıs ⁵ ob-l⸱tio ˡꝯ ⁵

2 The *Sacrifice* of the wicked is an abomination to the Lord, how much more when he bringeth it with a wicked mind? 21 27

3 To do juſtice and judgment, is more acceptable to the Lord than *Sacrifice* 21 3.

Safety.

1 The horſe is prepared againſt the day of battle, but *ſafety* is of the Lord 21. 31

Scorn.

1 A *ſcorner* ſeeketh wiſdom, and findeth it not; but knowledge is eaſie unto him that underſtandeth 14. 6

2 A *ſcorner* loveth not one that reproveth him, neither will he go unto the wiſe 15 12

3 Caſt out the *ſcorner*, and contention ſhall go out, yea ſtrife and reproach ſhall ceaſe 22 10

4 *Scornful* men bring a city into a ſnare, but wiſe men turn away wrath. 29 8.

5 When the *ſcorner* is puniſhed, the ſimple is made wiſe, and when the wiſe is inſtructed, he receiveth knowledge 21 11

6 He (the Lord) ſcorneth the *ſcorners*, but he giveth grace to the lowly 3 34

7 The thought of fooliſhneſs is ſin, and the *ſcorner* is an abomination to men. 24. 9

Seed

1 In the morning ſow thy *Seed* and in the evening with-hold not thy hand, for thou knoweſt not whether ſhall proſper, either this or that, or whether they both ſhall be alike good *Eccleſ* 11 6

Silver.

1 He that loveth *ſilver* ſhall not be ſatisfied with *Silver* nor he that loveth abundance, with increaſe *Eccleſ* 5 10

Servant.

2 Sacrificum ⸗ improbus ¹ ſum ¹³ ꝛbominatio ⸗⁵Jehova , quanto magis cum ⁷ offero ⁶⧾⸗ ille ⸗ ſceleratus ²⁹ animus ? 21 27.

3 Exerceo ⁶ juſtitia & ³² jus ¹² ſum magis ¹⁴ dilectus ²² Jehova, quam ²⁵ ſacrificium 21 3

Safety.

1 Equus ¹ aptor ad dies ² prœlium, ſed ſalus jam a Jehova 21 31

Scorn.

1 Deriſor ¹ quœro ⁶ ſapienꞇ a, nec ⁷ invenio ⁴ is, autꞇn ſcientia ¹ ſum ¹⁴ facilis ²² pru-ꞇ ꞇ 14 3

2 Deriſor ¹ diligo non ⁶⧾³ ille qui ⁹ corr⸗ pio ¹³ ipſe, nec ⁷ adeo ad ſapiens ꞇs 12

3 Ejꞇio ⁶ deriſor, ſimulꝗ contentio ¹ exeo, ¹⁰ litigium & ²⁵ ignominꞇa ²⁰ ceſſo ²² 10

4 Deriſor ¹ duco ⁶ urbs in inſidiœ at ſapiens ꞇerto ⁶ irꞇ 29 8

5 Quum deriſor ¹ mulctor fatuus reſipiſco & quum ſapiens ¹ inſtruor, ꞇ percipio ⁶ ſcientia 21 11

6 ⸗ Ipſe (Jehova) ¹ derideo ⁶ deriſor, autꞇm du ¹ gratia ²⁵ manſuetus 3 34

7 Cogitatio ² ſtultitia ¹ ſum ¹³ peccatum, & deriꞇr ¹ ſum ¹ abominatio ⁴ homo 14 9

Seed.

1 Mane ⁵ ſero ꞇ tuus ⁶ ſemen, & ¹⁹ veſper ne ⁵ remitto ꞇ tuus ⁶ manus, nam ⁵ ignoro ³ uter ¹ floreo ⸗ hiccine an ³ ille, ſive is ³ ambo ſum pariter ¹⁴ bonus Eccleſ 11 6.

Silver.

1 Qui ¹ amo ⁶ pecunia, non ⁷ ſatior ⁸ pecu-ria, nec qui ¹ amo ⁶ abundantia, ⁸ proventus Eccleſ 5 10

F 2   Servant.

Servant.

1 Accuse not a *servant* unto his Master, lest he curse thee and thou be found guilty 30 10

2 A wise *servant* shall have rule over a son that causeth shame and shall have part of the inheritance among the Brethren 17 2

3 The King's favour is towards a wise *servant*, but his wrath is against him that causeth shame. 14 35

4 He that delicately bringeth up his *servant* from a child, shall have him become his son at length 29 21.

Slothful.

1 The *slothful* man saith, there is a Lion in the way, a Lion is in the streets .6 13

2 The *slothful* man hideth his hand in his bosom, and it grieveth him to bring it again to his mouth 26 15

3 The *sluggard* is wiser in his own conceit, than seven men that render a reason 26. 16

4 As the door turneth upon the hinges, so doth the *slothful* man upon his bed 26 14

5 The desire of the *slothful* killeth him, for his hands refuse to labour 21 25

6 He that is *slothful* in his work, is brother to him that is a great waster 18 9

7 I went by the field of the *slothful* and by the vineyard of the man void of understanding, and lo! it was all grown over with thorns, and nettles had covered the face thereof, and the stone wall thereof was broken down 24. 30, 31

8. By much *slothfulness* the building decayeth, and through idleness of the hands the house droppeth through *Eccles.* 10 18

9 The *sluggard* will not plow by reason of the cold, therefore shall he beg in harvest and have nothing. 20. 4

Servant.

1 Ne �ⁱ accuſo ⁶ ſervus apud ³ ſuus dom us,
... ⁷ maledico ¹¹ tu, & tu ⁱ peragor ⁴ reus 30 10

. Intelligens ſe vus ⁱ dominer in filius pudefaciens, & ¹⁰ paſtior ⁶ poſſeſſio inter frater.
ſ

; Rex benevolentia ⁱ ſum erga ⁰ intelligens
ſe us, autem - is furor ⁱ ſum contra ⁰ pudefac-
ens 14 35

; Q i delicate ⁹ educo ˙ ſuus ⁶ ſervus à pueritia, ⁷ reddo ⁶ + ⁰ is ˙ ſuus ⁶ filius tandem 19 21

Slothful.

1 Piger ⁱ dico, ⁱ ſum leo in via, leo ⁱ ſum in
platea 26 13.

. ⁰ ger ⁱ condo ſuus ⁶ manus in ⁰ ſuus gremium & doleo 24 reduco ⁶ + ⁰ is ad ſuus os 26 15.

, Piger ſum ſapientior in ⁰ ſuus oculus,
qu m ſeptem ²⁰ vir qui 9 poſſum 24 reddo ⁶ ra-
to 26 16

; Ut janua ⁱ circumagor in ⁰ ſuus cardo, ita
piger in ⁰ ſuus lectus ⁰6 14

; Deſiderium ² piger ⁱ occido ⁶ + ⁴ is, nam ² is
manus ⁰ renuo 24 laboro 21 25

6 ⁵ Qui ⁰ ſum 24 remiſſus ³ ſuus ˙ opus ˙ ſum
frater 45 diſcordens 18 9

7 ⁵ Tranſeo juxta ager - piger, & juxta vinea
- ro ⁰ demens, autem ecce, ⁰ totus ⁰ tegor
⁰ ſpina, & urtica ⁱ tego ⁶ ſuperficies ² is, & lapideus maceria - is ⁰ deſtruor 24 30, 31.

8 ⁰ Multus ⁴⁹ pigritia contignatio ⁱ attenuor
& ²⁹ demiſſio - manus domus ⁱ periſtilo Eut j.
10. 18

9 Piger non ⁱ aro propter hyems, idcirco
⁷ mendico in æſtas & ⁰ habeo nil. 20 4

10. As vinegar to the teeth, and as smoke to the eyes, so is the *sluggard* to them that send him. 10. 26.

Spirit.

1 The *spirit* of a man is the candle of the Lord, searching all the inward parts of the belly. 20. 27

2 Who knoweth the *spirit* of man that goeth upward, and the *spirit* of a beast that goeth downward to the earth *Eccles* 3. 21

3 As thou knowest not what is the way of the *spirit*, nor how the bones do grow in the womb of her that is with child, even so thou knowest not the works of God who maketh all *Eccles*. 11. 5.

4 There is no man that hath power over the spirit to retain the *spirit*, neither hath he power in the day of death, and there is no discharge in that war, neither shall wickedness deliver those that are given to it *Eccles* 8. 8

5. The *spirit* of a man will sustain his infirmity; but a wounded *spirit* who can bear? 18. 14.

Stones.

1 Whoso removeth *stones*, shall be hurt therewith, and he that cleaveth wood shall be endanger'd thereby *Eccles* 10. 9

Study.

1 Of making many books there is no end, and much study is a weariness of the flesh. *Eccles* 12. 12

Sun.

1 The thing that hath been, it is that which shall be, and that which is done, is that which shall be done, and there is no new thing under the *sun* *Eccles* 1. 9.

1². Ut acetum ⁴⁵dens, & velut ²³fumus
⁴⁾oculus, ita ¹fum piger ⁴⁵mittens ⁵¹⊢³ipſe.
10. 26

Spirit.

1. Anima ²homo ¹fum ⁵⁾lucerna ²Jehova,
⁵perveſtigans ³omnis ³¹penetrale ² venter 20 27.

2 Quis ¹animadverto ⁶ſpiritus humanus
qui ⁷aſcendo ſurſum, & ⁸ſpiritus ⁹qui ⁹de
ſcendo deorſum ad terra. Eccleſ. 3. 21

3 Quemadmodum ⁹ignoro ⁹qui ¹ſum ⁵via
ſpiritus, nec quemadmodum os ¹formor in
u⁴erus ²gravida, ita ⁵ignoro ⁵opus ²Deus
qui ⁹creo ⁶omnis Eccleſ 11 5

4 ¹Sum ³nullus homo qui ⁹dominor ¹⁶ſpiri
tus ut ⁷contineo ⁶ſpiritus neque ⁹⁾habeo ⁵do
minatio in dies ²mors, & ¹ſum nullus miſſio
in ⁷iſte prælium, nec impietas ¹libero ⁶⊢⁷is
qui ⁹ſum ¹⁴deditus ³¹⊢⁷is Eccleſ 8 8

5 Spiritus ²vir ¹ſuſtento ⁷ſuus ⁶ægritudo,
autem ⁵fractus ⁶ſpiritus quis ²⁴ſuſtento ¹poſ
ſum⁷ 18. 14

Stones.

1 Qui ⁹amoveo ⁶lapis, offendor ²⁹⊢⁷is,
& qui ⁹findo ⁶lignum ⁷periclitor ²⁰⊥³is.
Eccleſ 10. 9.

Study.

1 ⁵²Facio ³multus ³⁹liber ¹ſum ³nullus fi.
nis, & ³multus lectio ¹ſum ¹⁴fatigatio ²caro.
Eccl ſ. 12 12.

Sun.

1 Res ³qui ⁹ſum, ¹ſum ⁵idem ³qui ⁹ſum,
& ³is ³qui ⁹fio, ¹ſum ⁷idem ⁷qui ⁹fio, &
¹ſum nil ⁷novus ſub ſol Eccleſ. 1 9.

Strife.

1. The beginning of strife is as when one letteth out water, therefore leave off contention before it be meddled with. 7 4

2. The churning of milk bringeth forth butter, and the wringing of the nose bringeth forth blood, so the forcing of wrath bringeth forth strife 30 33

3 He loveth transgression that loveth strife, and he that exalteth his gate, seeketh destruction. 17. 9

4 Where no wood is there the fire goeth out so where there is no tale-bearer, the strife ceaseth. 26. 20.

5 A wrathful man stirreth up strife but he that is slow to anger appeaseth strife 15 18

6 He that passeth by and meddleth with strife, that belongeth not to him, is like one that taketh a dog by the ears. 26 17

Surety.

1. Be not thou one of them that strike hands, or of them that are sureties for debts, for if thou hast nothing to pay, why should he take away thy bed from under thee? 22 26, 27

2 A man void of understanding striketh hands, and becometh surety in the presence of his friend 17. 18.

3. Take his garment that is surety for a stranger, and take a pledge of him for a strange woman 20 16

4. My son, if thou be surety for thy friend, if thou hast stricken thy hand with a stranger, thou art snared with the words of thy mouth, thou art taken with the words of thy mouth 5 1, 2.

Strife.

1 Initium ²contentio ¹ſum quaſi cum qui ⁹laxo ⁶aqua, quare ⁵deſero ⁶lis antequam ¹agi-tor 17 14

2 Preſſura ²lac ¹educo ⁶butyrum, & preſ-ſura ²naſus ¹educo ⁶ſanguis, ita preſſura ²ira ⁵educo ⁶lis. 30 33

3 ⁷Diligo ⁶defectio, qui ⁹diligo ⁵jurgium, & qui ⁹amplio ⁼ſuus ⁶janua, ⁷quaero ⁶fractura. 17. 19

4 Ubi ³nullus lignum ¹ſum, ibi ignis ⁵ex-tinguor, ita ubi non ¹ſum ſuſurro, contentio ¹ſileo. 26 20.

5 ⁹Iracundus vir ¹unceo ⁶contentio, au-tem qui ⁹ſum tardus ad lia, ⁷ſedo ⁶lis 15 18.

6 Qui ⁹tranſeo, & ¹⁰excandeſco in lis non ⁵ſuus, ⁷ſum ¹⁴ſimilis ― ille qui ⁹prehendo ⁹canis ²⁹auris. 26 17

Surety.

1 Ne ⁵ſum ¹⁴unus ex ille ³qui ⁹ferio ⁶mag-nus, aut ex ille ³qui ⁵ſum ¹³ſponſor pro debi-tum, nam ſi non ¹ſum ¹¹tu ⁶qui ⁵reddo, quare ⁷accipio ³tuus ⁶cubile a tu? 22 26 27

2 Homo ³demens ¹complodo ⁶manus, & ⁰fio ¹³ſponſor ante ³ſuus amicus. 17. 18

3. ⁵Capio ²is ⁶veſtis ⁹qui ⁹ſpondeo pro ex-traneus, & ¹⁰accipio ⁶pignus ab is pro ³alie-nus mulier 20 16

4 ³Meus ²⁶filius, ſi ⁵ſpondeo pro ³tuus amicus, ſi ⁵complodo ³tuus ⁶manus cum ex-traneus, ⁵illaqueor ²⁹ſermo ³tuus ²os, ⁵capi-or ²⁹ſermo ³tuus ²os. 6. 1, 2.

5. He that is *furety* for a stranger fl all fmart for it, and he that hateth *fu exifhip*, is fure 11 15

Tale-bearer.

1 A *tal.-bearer* revealeth fecrets, but he that is of a faithful fpirit concealeth the matter 11 13

2 The words of a *t.l -bearer* are as wounds, and they go down into the innermoft parts of the belly 18. 8

3 He that goe h about as a *tale-brarer*, revealeth fecrets, therefore meddle not with him, that flattereth with his lips 20 19

Thief.

1. Whofo is partner with a *thief*, hateth his own foul, he heareth curfing, and bewrayeth it not. 29.

Thoughts.

1. The *thoug'ts* of the wicked are an abominat on to the Lord, but the words of the pure are pleafant words 15. 26.

2 Commit thy works unto the Lord, and thy *loughts* fhall be eftablifhed. 16 3

Time.

1 To every thing there is a feafon, and a *time* to every purpofe under the heaven *Ecclef* 3 1

2 A *time* to be born, and a *time* to die, a *time* to plant, and a *time* to pluck up that which is planted *Ecclef* 3. 2.

3 A *time* to kill, and a *time* to heal, a *time* to break down, and a *time* to build up. *Ecclef* 3. 3.

4 A *time* to caft away ftones, and a *time* to gather ftones together, a *time* to embrace, and a *time* to refrain from embracing *Ecclef* 3. 5.

5 Qui 9 spondeo pro extraneus 7 confringor, autem 3 qui 9 odi 6 sponsio, 7 sum 14 securus. 11 15

Tale-bearer.

1 Susurro 1 revelo 6 arcanum, at 3 qui 9 sum fidus 18 animus 7 tego 6 res. 11 13

2. Verbum 2 susurro 1 sum ut 2 vulnus, & 10 descendo in penetrale 2 venter 18 8

3 Qui 9 ambulo ut 2 susurro, 7 revelo 6 arcanum, ergo ne 5 commisceor cum ille 3 qui 9 adulor 3 suus 29 labium 20 19.

Thief.

1 Quicunque 1 partior cum fur, 7 odi 3 suus 6 animus, 7 audio 6 execratio, & non 10 indico 6 + 15 29 24

Thoughts.

1 Cogitatio 2 malus 1 sum 1 abominatio 45 Jehova, autem sermo 2 mundus 1 sum 3 amœnus 1 sermo 15 26.

2 5 Devolvo 3 tuus 6 factum in Jehova, & 3 tuus cogitatio 1 stabilior. 16 3

Time.

1 8 Quisque 45 res 1 sum occasio & 23 tempus 2 quisque 45 voluntas sub cœlu n Eccl^{es} 3 1.

2 Tempus 52 nascor, & 23 tempus 5 morior, tempus 52 planto & 23 tempus 1 extirpo 39 + 3 15 qui 9 sum 14 plantatus Ecclef 3 2

3. Tempus 5 occido, & 23 tempus 52 curo, tempus 52 diruo, & 23 tempus 52 ædifico Eccl^{es}. 3 3

4 Tempus 52 projicio 39 lapis, & 23 tempus 52 colligo 9 lapis, tempus 52 amplector, & 23 tempus 52 recedo ab amplexus. Ecclef 3 5.

5. Tem-

5 A *time* to get, and a *time* to lose, a *time* to keep, and a *time* to cast away *Eccles* 3 6

6. A *time* to rent, and a *time* to sew, a *time* to keep silence, and a *time* to speak *Eccles* 3 7.

7 A *time* to love, and a *time* to hate, a *time* of war, and a *time* of peace *Eccles* 3 8

Tongue

1 Death and life are in the power of the *tongue*, and they that love it, shall eat the fruit thereof 18 21

2 Whoso keepeth his mouth and his *tongue*, keepeth his soul from trouble 21 23.

3 A wholesom *tongue* is a tree of life but perverseness therein is a breach in the spirit. 15 4

4 She (a virtuous woman) openeth her mouth with wisdom, and in her *tongue* is the law of kindness 31 26

5. There is that speaketh like the piercing of a sword, but the *tongue* of the wife is health 12. 10

6 The north-wind driveth away rain, so doth an angry countenance a backbiting *tongue* 25 23.

7 He that hath a froward heart findeth no good, and he that hath a perverse *tongue* falleth into mischief 17 20

8 The *tongue* of the wife useth knowledge aright, but the mouth of fools poureth out foolishness 15 2

Tree

1 If the clouds be full of rain, they empty themselves upon the earth, and if the *Tree* fall towards the south, or towards the north, in the place where the *Tree* falleth, there shall it be *Eccles* 11. 3.

Truth.

5 Tempus ⁵² acquiro & ²³ tempus ⁵² perdo, tempus ⁵ servo & ²³ tempus ⁵² abjicio, *Ec* 3 6

6 Tempus ⁵² lacero & ²³ tempus ⁵ confuo, tempus ⁵² fileo & ²³ tempus ⁵² loquo . *Ecclef* 3 7

7 Tempus ⁵² amo & ²³ tempus ⁵⁰ odium ⁵² habeo, tempus ² bellum & ²³ tempus ² pax. *Ecclef* 3. 8

Tongue.

1 Mors & ²³ vita ⁵⁰ fum in poteſtas ² lingua, & qui ⁹ amo ⁶ ꜩ³ is ⁷ comedo ⁶ fruꜩus ² is. 18 21

2 Qui ⁹ obfervo ³ fuus ⁶ os & ³ fuus ²³ lingua, ⁷ confervo ³ fuus ⁶ anima ab anguſtia 21. 23.

3 ³ Salutifer lingua ⁷ fum ¹³ arbor ² vita, autem perverfitas in ³ is fum ¹³ confraꜩio in ſpiritus. 15 4

4 ³ Ill₌ (³ probus fœmina) ¹ aperio ³ fuus ⁶ os ²⁹ fapientia, & ² is ¹⁷ lingua ¹ infideo doꜩrina ² benignitas 31. 26.

5 ² Sum ⁵ qui ⁹ pronuncio ³ fimilis ²² tranffoffio ² gladius, at lingua ² fapiens ¹ fum ¹³ medicina. 12. 18

6 Boreas ¹ difpello ⁶ pluvia, ita ³ indignabundus vultus ³ obtreꜩans ⁶ lingua. 25 23

7 ¹¹ Qui ¹ fum ³ perverfus animus, ⁷ confequor non ⁶ bonum, & ¹¹ qui ¹ fum ³ verfutus lingua, ⁷ incido in malum. 17. 20.

8 Lingua ² fapiens ¹ utor ⁴⁷ fcientia bene, autem os ² ſtolidus ¹ eruꜩo ⁶ ſtultitia 15 2.

Tree.

1. Si nubes ¹ fum ¹⁴ repletus ⁴⁰ pluvia, ¹ demitto ⁶ fui fuper terra, & fi arbor ¹ decido ad meridies, five ad aquilo, ¹⁹ locus ubi arbor ¹ cado, ibi ¹ fum ³ futurus *Ecclef* 11 3.

Truth.

U

Truth.

1 My mouth shall speak *Truth*, and wickedness is an abomination to my lips 8 7

2 Buy the *Truth*, and sell it not, also wisdom and instruction, and understanding 23 23

Trust.

1 *Trust* in the Lord with all thy heart, and lean not to thy own understerstanding 3 5

Vanity.

1 He that soweth *vanity*, shall reap *vanity*, and the rod of his anger shall fail. 22 8.

Violence.

1. They (the wicked and evil men) eat the bread of wickedness, and drink the wine of *violence* 4 17.

2 A man that doth *violence* to the blood of any person, shall flee to the pit, let no man stay him 28 17

3 A *violent* man enticeth his neighbour, and leadeth him into a way that is not good 16. 29

Understanding.

1 Happy is the man that findeth wisdom, and the man that getteth *understanding* 3. 13.

2 Wisdom is the principal thing, therefore get wisdom; and with all thy gettings get *understanding* 4 7.

3 How much better is it to get wisdom than gold? and to get *understanding*, rather to be chosen than silver? 16 16

4 *Understanding* is a well-spring of life to him that hath it, but the instruction of fools is folly. 16. 22

5 Good *understanding* giveth favour, but the way of transgressers is hard 13 15

6 Discretion shall preserve thee, *understanding* shall keep thee. 2 11.

Truth.

¥ 3 Meus palatum ¹ effero ⁶ veritas, & improbitas ¹ sum ¹⁹ abominatio ² meus ⁴⁵ labium 8 7.

2 ⁵ Comparo ⁶ veritas ac ne ⁵ vendo, etiam
-³ sapientia, & ²³ eruditio & ²⁰ prudentia 23 23.

Trust.

1 ⁵ Confido in Jehova ex ⁰ totus ³ tuus ſani-
mus, vero ne ⁵ innitor ³ tuus ¹⁷ intelligentia 3 5.

Vanity

1 Qui ⁹ ſemino ⁶ vanitas, ⁷ meto ⁶ vanitas,
& virga ⁰ ſuus ² furor ¹ deficio 22 8

Violence.

1 ³ Ille (³ improbus & ⁰ malus vir) ¹ comedo
⁶ cibus ² improbitas, & ¹⁰ bibo ⁶ vinum ² violentia 4 17

2 Homo ³ qui ⁹ exerceo ⁶ violentia in ſan-
guis ⁵ ullus ² homo, ¹ fugio ad fovea, ne quis
¹ moror ⁶+⁵ is. 28 17

3 ³ Violentus vir ¹ pellicio ³ ſuus ⁶ proximus,
& ¹⁰ duco ⁶+⁵ is in via ⁰ iniquus. 16 29

Understanding.

1 ¹⁴ Beatus ¹ ſum homo ³ qui ⁹ conſequor
⁶ ſapientia, & ²³ homo ³ qui ⁹ obtineo ⁶ intelligentia 3 13.

2 Sapientia ¹ ſum ³ præcipuus ¹⁰ res, ideo ⁵ acquiro ⁶ ſcientia, & cum ⁰ totus ⁰ tuus acquiſio
⁵ acquiro ⁶ prudentia 4 7.

3 Quanto ¹⁴ melior ¹² ſum comparo ⁶ ſapientia, quam ²³ aurum ? Et ¹⁰ comparo ⁶ prudentia ⁵ optatior ¹⁵ argentum ? 16 16

4 Intelligentia ¹ ſum ¹³ ſcaturigo ² vita ²¹ poſſidens ³¹+⁵ ipſe, at eruditio ² ſtultus ¹ ſum
¹⁰ ſtultitia 16 22

5 ³ Rectus intelligentia ¹ do ⁶ gratia, autem
via ⁵ perfidioſus ſum ¹⁴ aſper. 3 15

6 Solertia ¹ conſervo ⁶ tu, intelligentia ¹ cuſtodio ⁶ tu. 3. 21.

7 He that getteth wifdom, loveth his own foul, he that keepeth *underftanding*, fhall find good 19. 8.

8. The man that wandereth out of the way of *underftanding*, fhall remain in the congregation of the dead 21. 16.

9 Say unto wifdom, thou art my fifter, and call *underftanding* thy kinfwoman 7. 4

10 There is no wifdom, nor *underftanding*, nor counfel againft the Lord 21 30

Ungodly.

1. An *ungodly* man diggeth up evil, and in his lips there is a burning fire 16 17

Unjuft.

1 He that by ufury and *unjuft* gain increaf. eth his fubftance, he fhall gather it for him that will pity the poor 28 8

2 An *unjuft* man is an abomination to the juft, and he that is upright in the way, is abomination to the wicked 29 27

Upright.

1. God hath made man *upright*, but they have fought out many inventions, *Ecclef* 7 29

2 They that are of a froward heart, are abomination to the Lord, but fuch as are *upright* in their way, are his delight 11 20.

3 The high-way of the *upright* is to depart from evil, he that keepeth his way, preferveth his foul 16 17.

4 He that walketh in his *uprightnefs*, feareth the Lord, but he that is perverfe in his ways, defpifeth him 14. 2.

5 He that walketh *uprightly*, walketh furely, but he that perverteth his ways fhall be known 10 9

6 The way of the Lord is ftrength to the *upright*, but deftruction fhall be to the workers of iniquity. 10 29   7 He

7 Qui ˙ poſſideo ⁶ ſapientia, ⁷ diligo ⁵ ſuus
˙anima, qui ⁹ obſervo ⁶ intelligentia, ⁷ conſequor ⁶ bonum ˙9. 8.

8 Homo ⁵ qui ⁹ abberro à via ²intelligentia,
˙quieſco in cœtus ²mortuus 21 16.

9 ⁵ Dico ¹⁶ ſapientia tu ˈ ſum ⁵ meus ¹³ ſoror,
& ˈ voco ⁶ prudentia ⁵ tuus ⁵⁸ affinis. 7. 4

10. ˈ Sum ⁵ nullus ſapientia, nec ⁺⁵ intelligentia, nec ²⁵ conſilium adverſus Jehova 21 30.
Ungodl y.
1 ⁵ Nequam vir ˈ effodio ⁶ malum, & ² is
latium ˈ inſideo ⁵ adurens ignis. 16 17.
Unjuſt.
1 Qui ²⁹ fœnus & ⁵ injuſtus ²³ lucrum ⁹ augeo ⁵ ſuus ⁶ ſubſtantia, ⁷ congrego ⁶⁺⁵ is pro
ille qui ⁵ largior ²⁵ tenuis. 28 8

2 ⁵ Iniquus vir ˈ ſum ⁵³ abominatio ⁴⁵ juſtus & qui ⁹ ſum ¹⁴ rectus in via ⁷ ſum ⁵ abominatio ⁴⁵ improbus 29 27.
Upright.
1. Deus ˈ facio ⁶ homo ⁵ rectus, autem ⁵ ipſe quæro ⁵ plurimus ⁶ ratiocinium Ec 7. 29

2 Qui ⁹ ſum ⁵ perverſus ¹⁸ animus ˈ ſum
⁵ abominatio ⁴⁵ Jehova, at qui ⁹ ſum ¹⁴ integer
in ⁵ ſuus via ⁷ ſum ² ille ⁵ oblectatio 11 20

3 ¹³ Iter ² juſtus ¹² ſum recedo à malum, qui
⁵ cuſtodio ⁵ ſuus ⁶ via ⁷ conſervo ⁵ ſuus ⁶ anima 16 17

4 Qui ⁹ ambulo in ⁵ ſuus integritas ⁵ revereor
⁶ Jehova, vero qui ⁹ ſum ¹⁴ perverſus in ⁵ ſuus
via ⁷ ſperno ⁶⁺⁵ is. 14 2.

5 Qui ⁹ ambulo integre, ⁷ ambulo ſecure,
autem qui ⁹ perverto ⁵ ſuus ⁶ via ⁷ innoteſco.
10 9

6 Via ² Jehova ˈ ſum ¹³ robur ²¹ integer,
autem contritio ˈ ſum ²¹ operarius ² iniquitas.
10 29.   7. ⁵ Ille

7 He (the Lord) layeth up found wifdom for the *righteous*, he is a buckler to them that walk uprightly **2** 7.

8 A wicked man hardeneth his face, but as for the *upright* he directeth his way. 21. 29

9. Whofo walketh *uprightly* fhall be faved, but he that is perverfe in his ways, fhall fall at once 11. 13.

Vow.

1 It is a fnare to the man that devoureth that which is holy, and after *vows* to make enquiry 20 25

Water.

1 Stolen *waters* are fweet, and bread eaten in fecret is pleafant 9 17

Way.

1 There is a *way* that feemeth right unto a man, but the end thereof are the *ways* of death 14 12.

2. The *way* of the wicked is as darknefs, they know not at what they ftumble 4 19

3 The *way* of life is above to the wife, that he may depart from hell beneath. 15 24

4 Hear thou, my fon, and be wife, and guide thy heart in the *way*. 23 19

5. Man's goings are of the Lord, how can a man underftand his own *way*? 20 24

6 In all thy *ways* acknowledge him, and he fhall direct thy paths 3 6

7 Ponder the path of thy feet, and let all thy *ways* be eftablifhed. 4 26

8 He (the Lord) keepeth the paths of judgment, and preferveth the way of the faints 2. 8.

Wander.

1 As a bird that *wandereth* from her neft, fo is a man that *wandereth* from his place. 27 8.

7 ³ Ille (Jehova) ¹ repono ³ verus ⁶ fapientia pro rectus, ⁷ fum ¹³ fcutum ²¹ ambulans integre. 2 7

8 ³ Improbus vir ¹ obfirmo ³ fuus ⁶ facies, autem quod ad rectus ipfe ¹ apto ³ fuus ⁶ via. 21. 29.

9 Qui ⁹ ambulo integre ⁷ fervor, vero qui ⁶ fum ¹⁴ perverfus in ³ fuus via ⁷ cado fubito. 8 18

Vow.

1. ¹ Sum tendicula ²¹ homo ³ qui ⁹ deglutio ⁴ facrum, & poft ²⁰ voveo ¹⁰ inquiro 20. 25.

Water.

1 Aqua ³ furtivus ¹ fum ¹⁴ fuavis, & ²³ cibus ⁵ comeftus in latebræ ¹ fum ¹⁴ amœnus 9. 17.

Way.

1 ¹ Sum via ³ qui ⁹ videor ¹⁴ rectus ²¹ homo fed finis ² + ³ is ¹ fum ¹¹ via ² mors 14. 12.

2 Via ² improbus ¹ fum ¹⁴ fimilis -² caligo, ⁷ nefcio in quis ⁷ impingo. 4 19.

3 Iter ² vita ¹ fum furfum ²¹ intelligens, ut recedo a fepulcrum deorfum 15 24

4 ¹ Aufculto tu, ³ meus ²⁶ filius, & ¹⁰ fapio, ac ¹⁰ dirigo ³ tuus ⁶ animus in via 23 19

5 ² Vir egreffus ¹ fum à Jehova, quomodo ¹ poffum homo ergo ²⁴ intelligo ³ fuus ⁶ via ? 20. 24.

6 In ³ omnis ² tuus via ⁵ agnofco ⁶ + ³ is, & ipfe ¹ dirigo ³ tuus ⁶ iter 3 6.

7 ⁵ Expendo ⁶ orbita ³ tuus ² pes, & ³ omnis tuus via ¹ ftabilior 4 26

8 ⁵ Ille (Jehova) ¹ cuftodio ⁶ iter ² jus, & ¹⁰ confervo ⁶ via -fanctus 7. 8.

Wander.

1. Ut avicula ³ qui ⁹ erro à nidus ³ fuus, ita ¹ fum vir ³ qui ⁹ erro a locus ³ fuus 27 8.

Water.

1 Drink *water* out of thine own ciftern, and running *waters* out of thire own well. 5 15

2 Let thy fountains be difperfed abroad, and rivers of *waters* in the ftrees 5 16

3 The words of a mans mouth are as deep *waters*, and the well-fpring of wifdom as a flowing brook. 18 4

4 Caft thy bread upon the *waters*, for thou fhalt find it after many days *Ecclef.* 11. 1.

Weights.

1 Diverfe *weights* and diverfe meafures, both of them are alike abomination to the Lord, 20 10

2 Diverfe *weights* are an abomination to the Lord, and a falfe ba'ance is not good 20 23

3 A juft *weight* and balance are the Lords, all the *weights* of the bag are his work 16 11.

4 A falfe balance is an abomination to the Lord, but a juft *weight* is his delight 11 1

Wicked.

1 Enter not into the path of the *wicked*, and go not into the *way* of evil men 4 14

2 When the *wicked* cometh, then cometh alfo contempt, and with ignominy reproach 18 3

3. There fhall no evil happen to the juft, but the *wicked* fhall be filled with mifchief 12. 21

4 The foul of the *wicked* defireth evil, his neighbour findeth no favour in his eyes 21. 10.

5. His own iniquit's fhall take the *wicked* himfelf, and he fhall be holden with the cords of his fins 5 22.

6 Fret not thy felf becaufe of evil men, neither be thou envious at the *wicked* 24. 19

7. The

𝕎ater.

1 ⁵Bibo ⁶aqua e ³tuus cifterna & ²³fluen-
tum e ³tuus puteus 5. 15.

2 ³Tuus fons ¹fpargor paffim, & ²³rivus
²aqua in platea 5 16.

3 Verbum ⁵humanus ²os ¹fum velut ³pro-
fundus ²⁰aqua, & ²³fcaturigo ²fapientia ⁵fimi-
lis ³eructans ²²torrens. 18. 4.

4 ⁵Projicio ³tuus ⁶panis in aqua, nam ⁵in-
venio (+³is poft ³multus dies *Ecclef* 11 1.

𝕎eights.

1 ³Diverfus pondus & ³diverfus ²⁰menfura,
uterque ¹fum æque ¹³abominatio ⁴⁵Jehova.
20 10

2 ³Diverfus pondus¹ fum ¹³abominatio ⁴⁵Jehova, & ³dolofus lanx non ¹fum ³bonus 20 23.

3 ³Juftus trutina & ²⁰bilanx ¹fum ⁵⁹Jehova,
& ³omnis pondus ²loculus ¹fum ²is ¹³opus.
16 11.

4 ³Dolofus bilanx ¹fum ¹³abominatio ⁴⁵Jehova, vero ³integer pondus ¹fum ²+³is ¹.de-
l ctatio 11 1.

𝕎icked.

1 Ne ⁵ingredior ⁶iter ²improbus, neque
¹incedo per via ²malus 4 14

2 ⁵⁵Improbus ³adveniens, ¹advenio etiam
contemptus, & cum ignominia ²⁰probrum. 18 3

3. ⁵Nullus m leftia ¹evenio ²¹juftus, autem
improbus ¹impleor ⁸malum 12 21.

4. Animus ²improbus ¹defidero ⁶malum,
ipfe proximus non ¹invenio ⁶gratia in ²is oculus 21 10.

5. ³Suus iniquitas ¹capio ⁶improbus ³ipfe,
& ⁷teneor ²⁰funis ³fuus ²peccatum 5. 22.

6 ⁵Succenfeo ne propter maleficus, neque
¹invideo ²¹improbus 24 19.

7. Je-

7 The Lord hath made all things for himfelf, yea, even the *wicked* for the day of evil ·6 4

8. There shall be no reward to the evil man, the candle of the *wicked* shall be put out 24 20.

9 A good man obtaineth favour of the Lord, but a man of *wicked* devices will he condemn. 12 2

10 Be not afraid of fudden fear, neither of the defolation of the *wicked* when it cometh. 3. 25

11 The *wicked* fhall be cut off from the earth, and the trangreffor fhall be rooted out of it. 3, 22.

Wife.

1 Houfe and riches are the inheritance of fathers, but a prudent *wife* is from the Lord. 19. 14

2 Whofo findeth a *wife*, findeth a good thing, and obtaineth favour of the Lord 18 22.

3 Let thy fountain be bleffed, and rejoice with the *wife* of thy youth 5. 18

Wind.

1. He that obferveth the *wind* fhall not fow, and he that regardeth the clouds fhall not reap. *Ecclef.* 11 4.

Wine.

1. *Wine* is a mocker, ftrong drink is raging, and whofoever is deceived thereby is not wife. 20 1

2 Who hath woe? who hath forrow? who hath contentions? who hath babbling? who hath wounds without caufe? who hath rednefs of lips? they that tarry long at the *wine*, they that go to feek mixt *wine* 23. 29, 30.

7 Jehova [1] facio [6] omnis propter sui, imo, etiam [23] improbus ad dies [2] malum 16 4.

8 [1] Sum [3] nullus merces [21] malus, lucerna [2] improbus [1] extinguor 24. 20.

9 Bonus [1] adipiscor [6] benevolentia a Jehova, at [6] vir [5] sceleratus [18] machinatio [7] condemno. 32. 2

10 Ne [5] timeo a [3] repentinus pavor, nec a vastatio [2] improbus cum [1] advenio. 3 25

11 Improbus [1] excindor e terra, & perfidus [1] evellor ex [3] is 2. 22

Wife.

1. Domus & [23] divitiæ [30] sum [23] possessio [2] pater, autem [3] intelligens uxor [1] sum a Jehova. 19 14

2 Qui [9] consequor [6] uxor, [7] consequor [6] bonum, & [10] acquiro [6] benevolentia a Jehova 18 22.

3 [5] Tuus scaturigo [1] sum [14] benedictus, & [1] lætor de uxor [3] tuus [2] adolescent a 5. 18.

Wind.

1 Qui [9] observo [6] ventus non [1] sem no, & qui [9] respicio [6] nubes non [7] meto Eccles 11. 4.

Wine.

1 Vinum [1] sum [15] derisor & [3] inebrians po us am [14] tumultuosus, & quisquis [1] oberro in is, non [7] sapio 20 1

2 [1] Quis [1] sum calamitas? [11] quis [1] sum dolor? [11] quis [1] sum content o? [11] quis [1] sum loquacitas? [11] quis [1] sum vulnus impune? [11] quis [11] sum [3] ruber oculus? qui [9] immoror diu apud vinum, qui [9] eo [2] ad [20] investigo [3] mixtus [30] vinum 23 29 30.

Wise.

1 Bow down thine ear, and hear the words of the wise, and apply thy heart unto my knowledge 22 7

2 My Son if thy heart be wise, my heart will rejoyce, even mine 23 15

3 A *wise* man will hear, and will increase learning, and a man of understanding shall attain unto *wise* counsels. 1 5

4 In the multitude of words there wanteth not sin, but he that refraineth his lips is wise 10. 19.

5 The heart of the *wise* teacheth his mouth, and addeth learning to his lips 16 23

6 There is a treasure to be desired, and oyl in the dwelling of the *wise*, but a foolish man spendeth it up 21 22.

7 Go to the Ant, thou sluggard, consider her ways, and be *wise* 6 6

Wisdom.

1. I *wisdom* dwell with prudence, and find out knowledge of witty inventions 8 12

2 *Wisdom* is better than rubies, and all the things that may be desired, are not to be compared unto it 8 11.

3 *Wisdom* is better than weapons of war, but one sinner destroyeth much good Eccl 9 18

4 *Wisdom* is better than strength, nevertheless the poor man's *wisdom* is despised, and his words are not heard Eccl 9 16

5 *Wisdom* strengtheneth the wise, more than the mighty men which are in the city Ecc 7 19

6 *Wisdom* is too high for a fool, he openeth not his mouth in the gate 24

Wife.

1 ⁵Inclino ²tuus ⁴auris, & ¹⁰ausculto ⁶verbum ²sapiens & ¹⁰adhibeo ³tuus ⁴animus ad ⁵meus scientia 22. 17.

2 ⁵Meus ²⁶filius, si ²tuus animus ¹sapio, ³meus animus ¹lætor, etiam ³meus 2? 15

3 Sapiens ¹audio & ¹⁰adjicio ⁶disciplina, & homo ³intelligens ¹comparo ³industrius ⁶consilium 1 5

4 A multitudo ²verbum non ¹absum peccatum, sed qui ⁹cohibeo ³suus ⁶labium ¹sum ¹⁴sapiens 10 19

5 Animus ²sapiens ¹erudio ³suus ⁶os, & ⁰addo ⁶disciplina ²suus ¹⁷labium 16 23

6 ¹Sum thesaurus ²desideratissimus, & ⁻ oleum in habitaculum ²sapiens, autem ² stolidus homo ¹absorbeo ⁴⁺²ille 21 20

7 ⁵Adeo ad formica, O ⁻⁶piger, ²aspicio ⁺ ²s ⁶via & ¹⁰sapio 6.6.

Wisdom.

1 Ego ⁵⁷sapientia ⁴habito cum prudentia, & invenio ⁶scientia ²summas ²solertia 8 12

2 Sapientia ¹sum ¹⁴melior ¹⁵carbunculus, & omnis qui ⁴postea ⁻⁻ desidero non ¹sum grandis + is 8 11

3 Sapientia sum ¹⁴melior ¹⁵arma ²bellum, ⁻⁻ unus peccator ⁴perdo multus ⁶bonum &c. 9 18

4 Sapientia ¹sum ¹⁴melior ³robur, nihilominus ⁻ inopus sapientia ¹despicior, & ²is verbum non ¹audio Eccles 9 16

5 Sapientia ¹corroboro ⁶sapiens magis quam decem ²⁵dominator qui ⁹sum in civitas Eccl. 7 19

6 Sapientia ¹sum nimis ²altus ⁻¹ stultus, non ²aperio ²suus ⁶os in porta 24 7.

? Q-i

7. He that handleth a matter *wisely* shall find good, and whoso trusteth in the Lord, happy is he 16 20

8 Say not thou, what is the cause that the former days were better than these? for thou dost not enquire *wisely* concerning this *Ecclef.* 7 10

9 In much *wisdom* is much grief, and he that increaseth knowledge, increaseth sorrow. *Ecclef.* 1. 18,

Witness.

1 A faithful *witness* will not lye, but a false *witness* will utter lies 14 5

2 A false *witness* shall perish, but a man that heareth, speaketh constantly 21 28

3 A man that beareth false *witness* against his neighbour, is a maul, and a sword, and a sharp arrow 25 18

4. A true *witness* delivereth souls, but a deceitful *witness* speaketh lies. 14 25

5 An ungodly *witness* scorneth judgment, and the mouth of the wicked devoureth iniquity 19 28

6 Be not a *witness* against thy neighbour without cause, and deceive not with thy lips 24 28.

Woman.

1. A foolish *woman* is clamorous, she is simple and knoweth nothing 9 13.

2 The mouth of a strange *woman* is a deep pit, he that is abhorred of the Lord shall fall therein 22. 14

3. As a jewel of gold in a Swine's snout, so is a fair *woman* which is without discretion 11 22

4 A virtuous *woman* is a crown to her husband, but she that maketh ashamed, is as rottenness in his bones 12 4.

7 Qui 9 tracto 6 res sapienter 7 consequor 6 bonum, & qui 9 consilo 43 Jehova 14 beatus 1 sum 3 ille. 16 20

8 Ne 5 dico, 3 quis 1 sum causa quare 3 prior dies 1 sum 14 melior 15 +3 iste 7 nam non 5 rogo sapienter de hic. *Ecclef* 7. 10

9 In 3 multus sapientia 1 sum 3 multus indignatio, & qui 9 augeo 6 scientia, 7 augeo 6 dolor. *Ecclef.* 1. 18

Witneſs.

1 3 Fidus testis non 1 mentior, autem 3 falsus testis 1 efflo 6 mendacium 14 5

2. 3 Mendax testis 1 pereo, autem vir 7 qui 9 ausculto, 7 loquor in æternum 21 28

3. Vir 3 qui 9 testor 7 falsus 6 testimonium contra 3 suus proximus, 1 sum 13 marculus, & 25 gladius, & 7 acutus 23 sagitta 25 18

4 3 Verax testis 1 libero 6 anima, autem 7 dolosus testis 1 conflo 6 mendacium. 14 25.

5 3 Nequam testis 1 derideo 6 jus, & os 3 improbus 1 absorbeo 6 iniquitas. 19 28.

6 Ne 5 sum 13 testis contra 3 tuus proximus temere, neque 5 decipio 3 tuus 29 labium 24. 28.

Woman.

1 3 Stolidus mulier 1 sum 14 streperus, 7 sum 14 fatuus & 10 nosco 6 nihil 9 13

2 Os 3 extraneus 2 mulier 1 sum 3 profundus 13 fossa, 3 qui 9 sum 14 abominandus 59 Jehova 7 corruo in 3 ille 22 14.

3 Ut monile 3 aureus in rostrum 2 porcus, ita 3 sum 3 pulcher mulier 3 qui 9 sum sine prudentia 11. 22

4 3 Probus mulier 1 sum 13 corona 3 suus 23 maritus, sed 3 qui 9 pudefacio, 7 sum ut 23 putredo 21 ille 7 os. 12. 4.

3. 3 Quis

W

5 Every wife *woman* buildeth her house, but the foolish plucketh it down with her hands 14 .

6 It is better to dwell in a corner of the house-top, than with a brawling *woman* in a wide house 25 24

7 It is better to dwell in a wilderness, than with a contentious and an angry *woman* 21 19

8 Who can find a virtuous *woman*? for her price is far above rubies 31 10

9 One man among a thousand have I found, but a *woman* among all those I have not found Eccl 7 28

10 Favour is deceitful and beauty is vain, but a *woman* that feareth the Lord, she shall be praised 31 30

WORD.

1 Heaviness in the heart of man maketh it stoop, but a good *word* maketh it glad. 12. 25

2 Pleasant *words* are as honey-comb, sweet to the soul, and health to the bones 16 24

3 A *word* fitly spoken is like apples of gold in pictures of silver 25 1 .

FINIS.

5 ² Quiſque ² ſapiens mulier ¹ ædifico ³ ſuus
⁶ domus, autem ³ ſtultus ¹ deſtruo ⁶ + ² is ³ ſuus -⁹ m nus 14 ¹

6 ¹² Sum ¹⁴ melior habito in angulus ² tectum,
quam cum ² contentioſus mulier & in ³ commu-
n ² ¹⁰ ius 25 24

7 ¹² Sum ¹⁴ melior habito in deſertum, quam
cum ² contentioſus & ³ indignabundus mulier.
21 19

8 Quis ¹ invenio ³ probus ⁶ domina? nam ² is
pretium longe ¹ ſupero ⁶ carbunculus 31 10

9 ² Urus ⁶ homo inter mille ⁵ invenio, at
' fœmira inter ² omnus ² iſte non ⁵ invenio *Eccleſ.*
7. 28

10 Gratia ' ſum fallax & pulchritudo ¹ ſum
² vanus & mulier qui ⁹ revereor ⁶ Jehova, ³ ipſe ¹ laudor 31 30

Word.

1 Anxietas in animus - vir deprimo ⁶ + ³ ille, autem ² bonus verbum ¹ lætifico ⁶ + ² ille.
12 25

2. ³ Amœnus ſermo ¹ ſum ut ²² favus, ² dulcis
²² anima, & ²² ſilus ²¹ os 16 24

3 Verbum commode ³ dictus ¹ ſum ³ ſimilis
²² malum ² aureus in tabula ³ argenteus. 25 11.

FINIS.

REGULÆ SYNTAXEOS
Secundum LILL um,

Ad quas NUMERI *vocibus præfixi Tyronem referunt.*

ERBUM Perfonale cohæret cum nominativo numero & perfona , at verbum inter duos nominativos diverforum numerorum pofitum cum atlerutro convenire poteft.

Verbum perfonale *a verb perfonal* cohæret *agrees* cum nominativo *with the nominative cafe* numero *in number* & *and* perfona *in perfon* , at *but* verbum *a verb* pofitum *placed* inter duos nominativos *between two nominative cafes* diverforum numerorum *of different numbers,* poteft *may* convenire *agree* cum alterutro *with either of* them

2 Quum duo fubftantiva diverfæ fignificationis fic concurrunt ut pofterius a priore poffideri quodammodo videatur, tum pofterius in genitivo ponitur

Quum *when* duo fubftantiva *two fubftantives* diverfæ fignificationis *of different fignification* fic concurrunt

concurrunt *eo fo come together* ut *that* posterius *the latter* videtur *may seem* quodammodo *in some fort* possideri *to be possessed* a priore *by the former*, tum *then* posterius *the latter* ponitur *is put* in genitivo *in the genitive case*

3 Adjectivum cum substantivo casu genere & numero concordat, & ad eundem modum participia & pronomina substantivis annectuntur

Adjectivum *an adjective* concordat *agreeth* cum substantivo *with a substantive* casu *in case*, genere *in gender* & *and* numero *in number*, & *and* ad eundem modum *after the same manner* participia *participles* & *and* pronomina *pronouns* annectuntur *are joined* substantivis *to substantives*

4 Quæ significant partem temporis in ablativo frequentius usurpantur, in accusativo raro

Quæ *which* significant *signify* partem *a part* temporis *of time*, usurpantur *are used* frequentius *very often* in ablativo *in the ablative*, raro *seldom* in accusativo *in the accusative*

5 Nominativus primæ vel secundæ personæ rarissime exprimitur nisi causa discretionis aut emphasis gratia

Nominativus *the nominative case* primæ vel secundæ personæ *of the first or second person*, rarissime exprimitur *is very seldom expressed* nisi *except* causa discretionis *for difference sake*, aut *or* emphasis gratia *for the better expressing the thing to be spoken of*

6 Verba transitiva cujuscunque generis, sive activi sive communis, sive deponentis exigunt accusativum

Verba transitiva *verbs transitive* cujuscunque generis *of what kind soever*, sive *whether* activi *active* sive *or* communis *common*, sive *or* deponentis *deponent*, exigunt *require* accusativum *the accusative case*.

7. In

- In verbis quorum significatio ad homines tantum pertinet, tertia persona nominativus sæpe sub auditur

In verbis or verbs quorum significatio whose signification pertinet belongeth tantum only ad homines to men nominativus the nominative tertia personæ of the third person sæpe oftentimes subauditur is understood

8 Verba abundandi, impendi, onerandi & his diversa ablativo gaudent

Verba verbs abundandi of abounding impendi of spending, onerandi of loading, & and diversa contrary his to them gaudent govern ablativo an ablative case.

9 Quoties nullus nominativus interseritur inter relativum & verbum, relativum erit verbo nominativus, at si nominativus relativo & verbo interponatur, relativum regitur a verbo aut ab alia dictione, quæ cum verbo in oratione locatur

Quoties as often as nullus nominativus no nominative case interseritur is put inter between relativum the relative & and verbum the verb, relativum the relative erit shall be nominativus the nominative case verbo to the verb, at but si if nominativus a nominative case interponatur be put between relativo the relative, & and verbo the verb, relativum the relative regitur is governed a verbo of the verb, aut or ab alia dictione by another word quæ which locatur is placed cum verbo with the verb in oratione in the sentence

10 Conjunctiones copulativæ & disjunctivæ aliquoties similes modos & tempora conglutinant

Conjunctiones copulativæ conjunctions copulative & and disjunctivæ disjunctive aliquoties sometimes conglutinant join together similes modos like moods & and tempora tenses,

11 Est

11. Eſt pro habeo dativum exigit

Eſt pro habeo *when it ſignifies to have,* exigit *re-
quires* dativum *a dative caſe*

12 Non ſemper vox caſualis eſt verbo nominativus, ſed aliquando ve bum infinitum, aliquando oratio & aliquando adverbium cum
genitivo

Vox caſualis *a word declined with caſes* non eſt u-
n t ſempe *always* nominativus *the nominative
caſe* verbo *to the verb,* ſed *but* aliquando *ſom-
times* verbum infinitum *a verb of the infinitive
mood,* aliqua do *ſometimes* oratio *a ſentence,* aliqua do *ſometimes* adverbium *an adverb* cum genitivo *with a genitive caſe*

13 Verbi ſubſtantiva ut ſum, forem, fio, exiſto,
verba vocandi paſſiva ut nominor, appellor, dicor, vocor, nuncupor, & iis ſimilia ut ſcri-
bo ſalutor, habeor, exiſtimor item verba geſtus ut ſedeo, dormio, cubo, incedo, curro, utrim-
que nominativum expetunt.

Ve a ſubſtantiva *verbs ſubſtantive,* ut *as* ſum *I am,*
f rem *I might be,* fio *I am made* exiſto *I am,*
ve a paſſiva *verbs paſſive* vocandi *of calling,* ut
as nomiror *I am named* appellor *I am called,*
dicor *I am ſaid,* Vocor *I am called,* nuncupor
I am named, & *and* ſimilia *like iis to them,* ut
as ſcribor *I am written,* ſalutor *I am ſaluted,*
habeor *I am accounted,* exiſtimor *I am eſteemed,*
item *likewiſe* verba *verbs* geſtus *of geſture,* ut
as ſedeo *I ſit* dormio *I ſleep,* cubo *I lie down,*
incedo *I go,* curro *I run,* expetunt *require* nominativum *a nominative* utrinque *both before and
after them*

14 Denique omnia fere verba poſt ſe nominativum habent adjectivi nominis, quod cum ſup-
poſito verbi caſu genere & numero concordat

Denique

Denique *finally*, fere *commonly* omnia verba a *all*
verbs habent *have* post se *after them* nominativum *a nominative case* adjectivi nominis *of a*
noun adjective, quod *which* concordat *agrees*
cum supposito *with the nominative case* verbi *of*
the verb, casu *in case*, genere *in gender* & *and* numero *in number*

15 Comparativa cum exponuntur per quam ablativum adsciscunt

Comparativa *adjectives of the comparative degree*,
cum *when* exponuntur *they are expounded* per *by*
quam *than* adsciscunt *govern* ablativum *an ab-*
lative case

16 Verba imperandi & nunciandi dativum requirunt

Verba *verbs* imperandi *of commanding* & *and* nunciandi *of shewing*, requirunt *require* dativum *a*
dative case

17 Dativum postulant verba composita cum adverbiis bene, satis, & male, & cum his præpositionibus præ, ad, con, sub, ante, post, ob, in, inter.

Verba *Verbs* composita *compounded* cum adverbiis
with these adverbs, bene, satis, & male, & *and*
cum his præpositionibus *with these prepositions*,
præ, ad, con, sub, ante, post, ob, in, inter.
postulat *require* dativum *a dative case*

18 Laus & vituperium rei variis modis effertur,
at frequentius in ablativo vel genitivo

Laus *the praise* & *and* vituperium *the dispraise* rei
of a thing, effertur *is used* variis modis *divers ways*,
at *but* frequentius *more commonly* in ablativo *in*
the ablative case, vel *or* genitivo *the genitive case*

19 Præpositio subaudita interdum facit u addatur ablativus

Præpositio *a preposition* subaudita *being understood*
interdum *sometimes* facit *causes* ut *that* ablativus
an ablative case addatur *be added*

20 Gerundia

20 Gerundia in dum pendent ab his præpositionibus, inter, ante, ad, ob, propter

Gerundia *Gerunds* in dum pendent *do depend* ab his
præpositionibus *upon these prepositions*, inter, ante, ad, ob, propter.

21 Omnia verba acquisitive posita adsciscunt
dativum ejus rei cui aliquid quocunque modo
acquiritur, item verba significantia commodum
aut incommodum regunt dativum

Omnia verba *a'l verbs* posita *put* acquisitive *ac-
quisitively* adsciscunt *govern* dativum *a da...*
case ejus rei *of that thing* cui *wh... unto* aliquid
something acquiritur *is procured* quocunque modo
after what sort soever, item *likewise* verba *...*
significantia *sig fying* commodum *pi fit* aut *...*
incommodum *disprofit* regunt *govern* dativum *...*
dative cas

22 Adjectiva quibus commodum, incommodum
similitudo, dissimilitudo, voluptas, submissio,
aut relatio ad aliquid significatur in dativum
transeunt

Adjectiva *adjectives* quibus *where n* significatur
... fi d commodum *profit*, aut *or* incommodu
di profit similitudo *liken fs*, dissimilitud *...*
n... voluptas *pleasure*, submissio *submit ng* a
cr relatio *belonging* ad aliquid *to som thing* in d
tivum transeunt *govern... dative cale*

23 Conjunctiones copulativæ & disjunctivæ cum
his quatuor, quam, nisi, præterquam *...*, similes omnino casus nectunt

Conjunctiones copulativæ *conjunctions copula...*
and disjunctivæ *disjunctive*, cum his quatuor
with in se four, quam *than* nisi *exc pt*, præterquam *... that*, an *wh to r*, omnino nectunt
... og then join similes casus *like cases*

24 Quibusdam tum verbis tum adjectivis fami-
liariter subjiciuntur verba infinita

Verba

Verbi infinito *verbs of th infinitive mood* familia-
riter fubjiciuntur *are commonly put after* quibuf-
dam *fome* tum *both* verbis *verbs,* tum *and a'fo*
adjectivis *adjectives*

25 Verba dandi & reddendi regunt dativum

Verba *verbs* dandi *of giving* & *and* reddendi *of
reftoring,* regunt *govern* dativum *a dative cafe*

26 O exclamantis nominativo, accufativo & vocativo jungitur

O exclamantis, *an inter; ction if exclamation,* jungitur *is joined* nominativo *to a nominative cafe,*
accufativo *to an accufative cafe* & *and* vocativo
a vocative

27 Imperfonalia præcedentem nominativum non
habent

Imperfonalia *verbs imperfonal* non habent *have not*
nominativum *a nominative cafe* præcedentem
going before

28 His imperfonalibus fubjicitur accufativus cum
genitivo, pæniter, tædet, milere , miferefcit,
pudet, piget

Accufativus *an accufative cafe* cum genitivo *with a
genitive* fubjicitur *is put af er* his imperfonalibus
to fe imperfona', pæniter *it repen cth,* tædet *it
irk h o wearieth,* mileret *pit: th,* miferefcit
t hath compaf on on, pudet *i. fh meth,* piget *i.
grie b*

29 Quodvis verbum admittit ablativum fignificantem inftrumentum, aut caufam, aut modum
actionis

Quodvis verbum *any verb* admittit *admitteth* ablativum *an ablative cafe* fignificantem *fignifying*
inftrumentum *an inftrumen',* aut *or* caufam *the
cauf,* aut *or* modum *the manner* actionis *of doing*

30 Plures nominativi, fubfiantivi, vel antecedentia cujufcunque numeri poftulant verbum, adjectivum vel relativum pluralis numeri

Plures

Plures nominativi *many nominative cases*, substantivi *substantive* vel *or* antecedentia *antecedent* poʃʃunt requirere verbum *a verb*, adjectivum *an adjective* vel *or* relativum *a relative* pluralis numeri *of the plural number*

31 Participia regunt casus verborum a quibus derivantur

Participia *participle* regunt *govern* casus *the cases* verborum *of verbs* a quibus *from which* derivantur *they are derived*

32 Quæ autem durationem temporis aut continuationem denotant in accusativo, interdum & in ablativo efferuntur

Quæ autem *but nouns* which denotant *do signify* durationem *durance* aut *or* continuationem *continuance* temporis *of time* efferuntur *are used* in accusativo *in the accusative case* & *and* interdum *sometime* in ablativo *in the ablative*

33 Hæc impersonalia accusandi casum exigunt, juvat, decet, cum compositis, delectat, oportet

Hæc impersonalia *these verbs impersonal*, juvat *delighteth*, decet *it becometh*, cum compositis *with their compounds*, delectat *it delighteth*, oportet *it behoveth*, exigunt *require* accusandi casum *an accusative case*

34 Nomina partitiva, aut partitive posita, interrogativa quædam & certa numeralia genitivo, a quo & genus mutuantur, gaudent

Nomina partitiva *noun partitive*, aut *or* posita *put* partitive *partitively*, interrogativa quædam *certain interrogative*, & *and* certa numeralia *some nouns of number* gaudent genitivo *govern a genitive case*, a quo *of whom* & *also* mutuantur *they borrow* genus *their gender*

35 Verba infiniti modi pro nominativo accusativum ante se statuunt.

Verb.

Verbi *verbs* infiniti modi *of the infinitive mood*
ſtatuun ſet ante ſe *before hem* accuſativum *an
accuſative caſe* pro nominativo *inſtead of a nominative*

36 Infinitum quoque utrinque eoſdem caſus habet, præcipue cum verbi optand , eiſque ſimilia accedunt

Quoque *alſo* infinitum *a verb of the infinitive mood*
habet *hath* eoſdem caſus *the ſame caſes* utrinque
on either ſide, præcipue *eſpecially* cum *when* verba *verbs* optandi *of wiſhing* que *and* ſimilia *like
eis to them* accedunt *com new hem*

37 Forma vel modus rei adjicitur nominibus tum
ſubſtantivis, tum adjectivis in ablativo

Forma *the form* vel *or* modus *the manner* rei *of a
thing* adjicitur *is added* nominibus *to nouns* tum
both ſubſtantivis *ſubſtantives*, tum *and alſo* adjectivis *adjectives* in ablativo *in the ablative caſe*

38 Gerundia in do pendent ab his præpoſitionibus, a ab, abs, de, e, ex, cum, in, pro, &
ponuntur abſque præpoſitione.

Gerundia *Gerunds* in do pendent *do depend* ab his
præpoſitionibus *upon theſe præpoſitions*, a, ab, abs,
de, e, ex cum, in, pro, & *and* ponuntur *they
are put* abſque præpoſitione *without a præpoſition.*

39 Gerundia, ſive gerundivæ voces & ſupina regunt caſus ſuorum verborum

Gerundia *Gerunds* ſive *or* gerundivæ voces *words
like Gerunds*, & *and* ſupina *ſupines* regunt *govern*
caſus *the caſes* ſuorum verborum *of their own verbs.*

40 Adjectiva quæ ad copiam egeſtatemve pertinent interdum ablativo interdum & genitivo
gaudent.

Adjectiva *adjectives* quæ *which* pertinent *do belong*
ad copiam *to plenty* egeſtatemve *or want* interdum *ſometime* gaudent ablativo *govern an ablative caſe*, & *and* interdum *ſometime* genitivo *a
genitive.*

Verba

41 Verba obſequendi & repugnandi dativum regunt

Verba *verbs* obſequendi *of obeying* & *and* repugnandi
of reſiſting regunt *govern* dativum *a dative caſe*

42 Dignus, indignus, prædtus, captus, contentus, extorris, auferendi caſum exigunt

Dignus *worthy*, indignus *unworthy*, præditus *en-
dued*, captus *taken*, contentus *content*, extorris
baniſhed, exigunt *require* auferendi caſum *an*
ablative caſe

43 Verba fidendi dativum regunt

Verba *verb* fidendi *of truſting* regunt *govern* dativum *a dative caſe*

44 Verba ſignificantia commodum aut incommodum regunt dativum

Verba *verbs* ſignificantia *ſignifying* commodum *pro-*
fit aut *or* incommodum *diſprofit* regunt *govern*
dativum *a dative caſe*

45 Sum cum compoſitis præter poſſum exigit dativum

Sum, cum compoſitis *with his compounds* præter
except poſſum *I am able*, exigit *require,* dativum
a dative caſe.

46 Præpoſitio in compoſitione eundem nonnunquam caſum regit, quem & extra compoſitionem
regebat

Præpoſitio *a prepoſition* in compoſitione *in compoſition*
nonnunquam *ſometimes* regit *govern* eundem caſum *the ſame caſe* quem *which* & *alſo* regebat *it go-*
vern'd extra compoſitionem *without compoſion*

47 Fungor, fruor, utor, & ſimilia ablativo junguntur

Fungor *I do a duty*, fruor *I enjoy*, utor *I uſe* & *and*
ſimilia *ſuch like* junguntur *are joyned* ablativo *to*
an ablative caſe

48 Quibuſlibet verbis ſubjicitur nomen pretii in
ablativo caſu, & hi genitivi ſine ſubſtantivo
poſit

positi, tanti, quanti, pluris, minoris, tantidem, quan-
tivis, quantilibet, quanticunque sæpe annectuntur.

Nomen pretii *the word of price* subjicitur *is put af-*
quibuslibet verbis *any verbs* in ablativo casu
the ablative case, & *and* hi genitivi *these geni-*
tive cases positi *put* sine substantivis *without sub-*
stantives annectuntur *are join'd*, tanti *for so much*,
quanti *for how much*, pluris *for more*, minoris
for less, tantivis *so great as you list*, tantidem *for*
so much, quantilibet, *as great as may be*, quanticunque *how great soever*

49 Adjectiva regunt ablativum significantem
causam

Adjectiva *adjectives* regunt *govern* ablativum *an ab-*
lative case significantem *signifying* causam *the cause*

50 Prosequor te amore, laude, honore id est
amo, laudo, honoro, afficio te gaudio, supplicio, dolore, id est exhilaro punio, contristo

Prosequor te amore, id est *that is* amo *I love thee*,
prosequor te laude, id est *that is*, laudo *I praise*
thee, prosequor te honore, id est *that is* honoro
I honour thee, afficio te gaudio, id est *that is* exhilaro *I make thee merry* afficio te supplicio id
est *that is* punio *I punish thee*, afficio te dolore,
id est *that is* contristo *I make the sad*

51 Hei & væ dativo apponuntur

Hei, *alas* & *and* væ *alas* apponuntur *are put* dativo *to a dative case*

52 Gerundia in di pendent a quibusdam tum substantivis tum adjectivis

Gerundia *Gerunds* in di pendent *do depend* a quibusdam *upon some* tum *both* substantivis *substantives*,
tum *and also* adjectivis *adjectives*

53 Vestiendi verbi interdum mutant alterum accusativum in ablativum vel dativum.

Verba *verbs* vestiendi *of cloathing or arraying* interdum *sometime* mutant *change* alterum accusativum

tivum *the one accusative case* in ablativum *into an*
abla to vel *or* dativum *a dative*

54 Exosus & perosus etiam cum dandi casu leguntur videlicet passive significantia

Exosus *ha ed* & *and* perosus *hared unto death* etiam
also leguntur *are read* cum dandi casu *with a da-*
tive case videlicet *that is* significantia *signifying*
passive *passively.*

55 Quibuslibet verbis additur ablativus absolute
sumptus.

Ablativus *an ablative case* sumptus *taken* absolute
absolutely additur *is added* quibuslibet verbis *to*
any verb:

56 Adjectiva quæ desiderium, notitiam, memori
am atque iis contraria significant, genitivum
adsciscunt

Adjectiva *adjectives* quæ *which* significant *signify*
desiderium *dsire*, notitiam *knowledge*, memori-
am *remembrance* atque *and* contraria *things con-*
trary iis *to them* adsciscunt *govern* genitivum *a*
genitive case

57 Excipiuntur quæ in eodem casu per appositio
nem connectuntur.

Excipiuntur *nouns are excepted* quæ *which* connectuntur *are put together* in eodem casu *in the same*
case per appositionem *by apposition*

58 Sum genitivum postulat quoties significat pos-
sessionem aut ad aliquid pertinere

Sum postulat *requireth* genitivum *a genitive case*
quoties *as often as* significat *it signifieth* possessio-
nem *possession*, aut *or* pertinere *to belong* ad aliquid
to somewhat

59 Passivorum participia frequentius dativis gaudent

Participia *participles* passivorum *of verbs passive*
frequentius *very often* gaudent *govern* dativis
dative case:

INDEX

Nominum, Pronominum,
Verborum, & Participiorum,

QUÆ

In hoc OPERE *Continentur.*

A

 BDITUM, i, N S 2 D n g
Abeo, īvi, ii, īre, V. N. 4 Conj
ex ab & eo
Aberro, āvi, are, V. N. 1 Conj ex
ab & erro

Abjectio, ōnis, N S 3 D f g.
Abjectus, a, um, Part Præt ex abjicior
Abjicio, ēci, ĕre, V. A 3 Conj ex ab & jaceo
Abluo, ui, ĕre, V A 3 Conj ex ab & lavo.
Abluor, utus sum, ui, V P 3 Conj
Abominandus, a, um, Part Fut. ab abominor.
Abominatio. ōnis, N S 3 D. f g.

G   Abortivus.

Abortivus, a, um, N A 3 Term

Abrumpor, ptus fum, pi, V P 3 Conj ex ab &
   rumpor

Abfcondo, di, ĕre, V A. 3 Conj ex abs & co do.

Abfolvo, vi, ĕre, V A 3 Conj ex ab & folvo

Abforbeo, ũi & pfi, ĕre V A 2 Conj ex ab &
   forbeo

Abftergo, fi, ĕre, V A 3 Conj ex abs & tergo

Abundantia, æ N S 1 D f g

Abundo, āvi, āre, V. N. 1 Conj ex ab & undo.

Acetum, 1, N S 2 D n g

Accelero, āvi, āre, V A 1 Conj ex ad & celero

Accendo, di, ĕre, V A 3 Conj

Acceſſus, ũs, N S 4 D m g

Accipio, ēpi, ĕre, V A 3 Conj ex ad & capio

Accub tus, ũs, N. S 4 D. m g

Accurro, ri, ĕre V N. 3 Conj ex ad & curro

Accufo, āvi, are, V A 1 Conj ex ad & caufor

Acquiro, fivi, ĕre, V A 3 Conj ex ad & quæro

Acquiror, fitus fum, ri, V. P 3 Conj ex ad &
   quæror

Acquifitus a, um, Part Præt ab acquiror.

Acquifitio, ōnis, N S 3 D f g

Actio, ōnis, N S 3 D f g

Aculeus, 1, N S 2 D m g

Acuo, ui, ĕre, V A 3 Conj

Acutus, a, um, N. A 3 Term.

Addo, didi, ĕre, V. A 3 Conj ex ad & do

Adduco, xi, ĕre, V A 3 Conj ex ad & duco

Adeo, ivi, ire, V A 4 Conj ex ad & eo

Adhibeo, bũi, ĕre, V A 2 Conj ex ad & habeo

Adhibeor, itus fum, ēri, V P 2 Conj ex ad &
   habeor

Adjicio, jēci, ĕre, V A. 3 Conj. ex ad & jaceo.

Adipifcor, eptus fum, fci, V. D 3 Conj.

Admoneo,

Admoneo, ùi, ēre, V A. 2 Conj ex ad & moneo.

Adulteria, æ N S 1 D f g.

Adsum affui vel affui, adesse, V N ex ad & sum

Adveniens, tis, Part Præf ab advenio

Advenio, vēni, īre V N 4 Conj ex ad & venio.

Adversus, a, um, N. A 3 Term

Adverto, ti, ēre, V A 3 Conj ex ad & verto

Adulor, ātus sum, āri, V. D 1 Conj

Adultera, æ, N S 1 D f g

Adulterium ii. N S 2 D n g

Advoco, āvi, āre, V A 1 Conj ex ad & voco.

Adurens, tis, Part Præf ab aduro

Aduror, ustus sum, ūri, V P 3 Conj ex ad & uror.

Ædifico, āvi, āre, V A. 1 Conj ab ædes & facio

Ædificor, ātus sum āri, V P 1 Conj

Æger, ra, rum, N A 3 Term

Ægritudo, ïnis, N S 3 D f g

Æmulor, ātus sum, āri, V D 1 Conj

Æquandus, a, um, Par ab æquor

Æquitas, ātis, N S 3 D f g

Æquus, a, um, N A 3 Term

Ærumnosus, a, um N A 3 Term

Æstas, ātis, N S 3 D f g

Æstimor, ātus sum, āri, V P 1 Conj

Æternum, i, N S 2 D n g

Affectus, a, um, N A 3 Term

Affero, attuli, afferre, V A 3 Conj ex ad & fero.

Afficio, ēci, ēre, V. A 3 Conj ex ad & facio.

Affinis is N S. 3 D c g

Afflictio, ōnis N S 3 D f g

Afflictus, a, um, P Præt ab affligor.

Ager, gri, N S 2 D m g

Agitor, ātus sum, āri, V. P 1 Conj

Agnosco ōvi, ēre, V A 3 Conj. ex ad & nosco.

Agnoscor,

... o cor tus fu n, fc \ P ; Co)

' 'g c , V A ; Co)

\ , t uun V D

e N S D f g

Al   s, N S ; ; c g

Allerus, -, un, N A ; Term

Aliqu s N A ; \ J 4 Term

Alius, Alia, Aliud, N A ; Term

Alligor, ātus fum, āri, V P i Conj ex ad & li
gor

Alo, ui, ēre, V A ; Conj

Alter, a, um, N A ; Term

Altitudo. īnis, N S ; D f g.

Al or, ōris, N A ; Ait Comp

Altiffimus, a, um, N A ; Term Superl ab

Altus, a, um, N A ; Term

Amaritudo, īnis, N S ; D f g

Amarus, a um, N A ; Term

Ambo, orum, arum, orum, N A pl ; Term

Ambulans, tis, Part I ræf ab ambulo

Ambulo, āvi, āre, V. N i Conj

Amænitas, ātis, N S ; D f g

Amænus, a, um, N A ; Term

Amicitia, æ N S. i D f g

Amicus, i, N S ; D m g

Amo, āvi, āre, V A Conj

Amor, ōris, N S ; D m g

Amoveo, ōvi, ēre V A ; Conj ex a & moveo

Amplector, xus fum, &c V D ; Conj ex am &
plecto

Amplexus, ūs, N S 4 D m g

Amplifico, āvi, āre, V A. i Conj ex amplus.

Amplus, ior, iffimus N A ; Term

Angelus, i, N S ; D m g

Angulus, i N S ; D m g

Angustia, æ, N S i D f g

Angustus a, um, N A ; Term.

Anima,

Anima, æ, N S 1 D f g

Animadverto, ti, ēre, V A 3 Conj ex animus ad
   & verto

Animus, i, N S 2 D m g

Annus, i, N S 2 D m g

Antiquus, a, um N A 3 Term.

Anxietas, ātis, N S 3 D f. g

Aperio, ui, īre, V A. 4 Conj ex ad & pario

Apto, avi, āre V A 1 Conj

Aptor, ātus sum, āri, V P 1 Conj

Aqua, æ N S 1 D f g.

Aquila, æ, N S 1 D f g.

Aquilo ōnis, N S 3 D m g

Aratio, ōnis, N S 3 D f g

Arbor, ŏris, N S 3 D f g

Arcanum, i, N S 2 D n g

Ardens, tis Part Præf ab ardeo

Arena, æ, N S 1 D f g

Argenteus, i, um, N A 3 Term

Argentum, i, N S 2 D n g

Arma, ōrum, N S Pl 2 D n g.

Aro, āvi, āre V A 1 Conj

Arx, cis, N. S 3 D f g

Ascendo, di, ere, V. A 3 Conj ab ad & scando.

Asinus, i, N S 2 D m g

Aspectus, ûs, N S 4 D m g.

Asper, a, um, N. A 3 Term

Aspiciens, tis, Pars Præf ab

Aspicio xi, ēre, V A 3 Conj ex ad & specio

Applico, ūi & avi, āre, V. A 1 Conj ex ad &
   plico

Assequor, utus, qui, V D. 3 Conj ex ad & sequor

Asservātus, a, um, P Præt. ab asservor.

Asso, āvi, āre, V A 1 Conj

Associor, ātus sum, āri, V P. 1 Conj. ex ad &
   socior.

Assumo,

ATumo pfi. ěre V A 3 Conj ex ad & fumo

Aſto, titi ſtare, V A 1 Conj ex ad & ſto

Aſturus, um, N A 3 Term

Attendo di ěre V A 3 Conj ex ad & tendo

Attenuor ātus ſum, īri, V P 1 Conj ex ad & tenuor

Attero trītus ſum, ri, V P 3 Conj. ex ad & tero

Atto, ... es N A 2 Art

Atrinens, ... Parti... rif b

Audio, ivi, ir V A 4 Conj

Audior, īrostum īri V P 4 Conj

Auditio ōnis N S 3 D fg

Aveto, ti, ěre V A 3 Conj. ex a & tero

Augero abfuli, ſutere V A 3 Conj ex ab & tero

Augeo ... ěre V A 2 Conj

Avicula æ, N S 1 D f g

Avicul a um N A 3 Term

Avis s N S 3 D f g

Avolo a as, V A 1 Conj ab a & volo

Aurum um, N A 3 Term

Aura ... N ... 1 g

Auum, ... N S 3 D n g

Aufultens es ... Parti... ab

Aufculto av ire V 3 Conj

B

Bacilus, N 2 L m g

Balſis æ, N S 1 D f g

Beatu um N A 3 Term

Bellum i, N S ... n g

Benedico, ěre, V A 3 Conj ex bene & dico

Benedi r, ěuſ ſum, dici V P 3 Conj

Benedictio, ōnis, N S 3 D f g

Benedictus, a, um, N A 3 Term

Beneficus

Beneficus, a, um, N A 3 Term

Bene factus sum fieri, V N P ex bene & fio.

B evolentia, æ, N S 1 D f g

B ignitas, atis, N S 3 D f g

B gau, , um N A 3 Term

B , N S 1 D f g

bibi ěre, V N 3 Conj

B x, c , N S 3 D f g ibis & lans

B d or, i us sum iri, V D 4 Conj

B lus, um, N A 3 Term

B itas, tatis, N S 3 D f g

B um, i, N S 2 D n g

b us, a, um N A 3 Term

B rs, e, N S 1 D m g

P b N S 3 D c g

P tas, um, N A 3 Term

B ter, c, N S 1 D f g

Turtuta, i, N S 2 D n g

C

C Adens tis, Part Iras 3

C ado, cěcidi, ěre, V N 3 Conj

Calamitas, atis, N S 3 D f g

Caco av, re, V A 1 Conj a calx.

Calcu, i, um, N A 3 Term

Cho is, N S 3 D f g

Cnis, is, N S 3 D c g

Camies, ei, N S 5 D f g

Cno cěcini ěre, V N 3 Conj

ro avi, are, V A 1 Conj

Canicum, i, N S 2 D n g

Caper, pri, N S 2 D m g

C pio, cěp, ere, V A 3 Conj

Capior, cap us um, capi, V P 3 Conj

C par tis, N S 3 D n g

Carbo, ōnis, N S 3 D m g

Carbun-

Carbunculus · N S 2 D m g
Cardo, inis N S 3 D m g
Careo, ui, & cassus sum, ere, V Irr 2 Conj
Caro, carnis, N S 3 D f g
Castigo ā-i āre V A 1 Conj
Cav..., is, N S 4 D m g
Ca inus · N S 2 D m g
...ulus · N S 2 D m g
Casco, vi ere, V N 2 Conj
Cau a, æ, N S 1 D f g
Cæli s , um N A 3 Term
Ce ... s, a, um, N A 3 Term
Centum, N A Indecl
Cer x, icis, N S 3 D f g
Ce ., āvi, are V N 1 Conj
Ci a is, atis, N S 3 D f g
Ch ius a, um, N A 3 Term
Cib um, i N S 2 D n g
Cibu , i, N S 2 D m g
Circuma or, actus sum, āgi V P. 3 Conj ex
    circu n & agor
C steina, æ, N S 1 D f g
C itas ātis, N S 3 D f g
C mo, av. āre, V A 1 Conj
Cl mor, ōnis, N S 3 D m g
Claudus, a, um, N A 3 Term.
Ch pearus, a um, N A 3 Term
Cœlum, i, N S 2 D n g
Cœtus, ûs, N S 4 D m g
Cogitatio ōnis, N S 3 D. f g
Cogito, avi āre, V A 1 Conj
Cognosco, ōvi ēre, V. A 3 Conj ex con & nosco
Cognoscor, itus sum, sci, V P ex con & noscor
Cognoscendus, a, um, Part Præt a cognoscor
Cohibeo, ūi, ēre, V A. 2 Conj. ex con & habeo
Colo ūi, ēre, V A 3 Conj
Colligo, ēgi, ēre, V. A. 3 Conj. ex con & lego.
                                    Comedo,

Commisceor, mixtus, sum misceri, V. P 2 Conj ex con & misceor

Committo, si, ěre, V A 3 Conj ex con & mitto.

Commodans, tis, Part Præf a commodo.

Commodum, i, N S 2 D n g

Commodus a, um, N A 3 Term

Commoror, ātus sum, āri, V D 1 Conj ex con & mor r

Communis, is, N A 3 Art.

Comparo, āvi, āre, V A 1 Conj ex con & paro.

Compenso, āvi, āre, V A 1 Conj ex con penso

Compensor, ātus sum, āri, V P 1 Conj ex con & pensor

Complicatio, ōnis, N S 3 D. f g

Complodo, si, ěre, V A 3 Conj ex con & plaudo.

Concelor illus sum di, V P , Conj ex con & celo

Conclave, is, N S 3 D n g

Concupisco, ii, ěre, V A 3 Conj ex con & cupio

Condemno, avi, are, V A 1 Conj ex con & damno

Condo, didi, ěre, V A 1 Conj ex con & ao

Condono, avi are, V A 1 Conj ex con & dono.

Confero, tuli, ferre, V A Irr ex con & tero

Confiteor, ětus sum, eri, V P. 3 Conj ex con & fateor

Confido, fidi & fisus sum, ěre, V N P 3 Conj ex con & fido

Confirmor, ātus sum, āri, V P 1 Conj ex con & firmo

Conflo, āvi, āre, V A 1 Conj ex con & flo

Confractio, ōnis, N S 3 D f g

Confringor, fractus sum, frangi, V. P 3 Conj. ex con & frangor

Congredior,

Congredior ssus sum d, V D 3 Conj ex con
& gradior

Congregatio, ōnis N C 2 D f g.

Congredior, ssi āre V A 1 Conj ex con & grex

Conguno ui ĕre, V N 3 Conj

Conjicior, ctus īci, V P 3 Conj ex con &
jaceor

Conjunctior, ōris, N A. Comp 3 Art

Conjungo, xi, ĕre, V A 3 Conj ex con &
jungo

Conjungor, ctus sum gi, V P 3 Conj ex con
& jungor

Conquiesco, ēvi, ĕre, V N 3 Conj ex con &
quiesco

Conquiro, sivi, ĕre, V A 3 Conj ex con &
quæro

Consequor cutus sum, qui, V D 3 Conj ex con
& sequor

Conservo, avi, āre, V A 1 Conj ex con & servo.

Considero, avi, are, V A 1 Conj

Consiliarius, ii, N S 2 D m g

Consilium ii N S 2 D n g

Consisto, stiti ĕre, V N 3 Conj ex con & sisto

Consolator ōris N S 3 D m g

Conspectus, ûs, N. S 4 D m g.

Constituo, ui, ĕre, V A 3 Conj ex con & statuo.

Consultus, a um Part Præt a consulor

Consumo, psi, ĕre, V A 3 Conj ex con & su-
mo

Consumor, ptus, mi, V P 3 Conj ex con & su-
mor

Consuo, ui, ĕre V A 3 Conj ex con & suo

Contemno, psi, ĕre, V A 3 Conj ex con &
temno

Contemnor, ptus sum, ni, V. P 3 Conj ex con
& temnor

Contempt...

Contemptus, ûs, N S 4 D m g
Contendo di, ĕre, V A 3 Conj ex con & tendo
Contentio ōnis, N S 3 D f g
Content osus, a, um, N A 3 Term
Contero, trīvi ĕre, V A 3 Conj ex con & tero
Contignatio, ōnis, N S 3 D f g
Contineo ui, ēre, V A. 2 Conj ex con & teneo.
Continuus, a, um, N A 3 Term
Contritio, ōnis, N S 3 D f g
Contumax, acis, N A 3 Art
Contundo, tŭdi, ĕre, V A 3 Conj ex con &
    tundo
Conturbatus, a um, Part Præf a conturbor
Conturbo, avi, are, V A 1 Conj ex con & turbo
Conturbor, atus fum, ari, V P 1 Conj ex con &
    turbor
Contufio, ōris, N S 3 D f g
Convenio, veni, ire, V N 4 Conj ex con &
    venio
Converto, ti, ĕre, V A 3 Conj ex con & verto
Convitior, atus fum, ari, V. D 1 Conj.
Convitium, ii, N. S 2 D n g
Convivium, ii, N S 2 D n g.
Copia, æ, N S 1 D f g.
Cor, dis, N S 3 D n g.
Cordatus, a, um, N A 3 Term.
Corona, æ, N S. 1 D f g
Correctio, ōnis, N S 3 D f g
Correptio, ōnis, N S 3 D f g
Correptus, a, um, Part Præt a Corripior
Corrigo, xi, ĕre, V A. 3 Conj ex con & rego
Corripio, ui, ere, V A 3 Conj ex con & rapio
Corroboro, avi, are, V A. 1 Conj ex con & ro-
    boro
Corrumpo, pi, ĕre, ex con & rumpo.
Corrumpor, ruptus fum, rumpi, V. P. 3 Conj.
    ex con & rumpo.

Corruptus,

Corruptus, a, um, Part i ae a Corrup por

Corrue, ui, ĕre, V N 3 Conj ex con & ruo

Corvus, i, N S 2 D m g

Craftinus, a, um, N A 3 Term

Creator ō is, N S , D m g

Credo, didi, ĕre, V A 3 Conj

Creo, vi, are, V A 1 Conj

Crepitus, us, N S 4 D m g

Cresco cui ĕre V N 3 Conj

Crudelis is, N A 3 Air

Cubile, is N S 3 D n g

Culter tri N S 2 D m g

Cultura æ, N S 1 D f g

Cupedia, arum, N S 1 D f g

Curatio, ōnis, N S, D f g

Curo, avi, are V A 1 Conj

Curfus, ûs, N S 4 D m g

Cuftodio, ivi, ire V A 4 Conj a cuftos

D

DEbeo ui, ĕre, V A 2 Conj ex de & habeo

Debitum, i, N S 2 D n, g

Debitus a, um, N A 3 Term.

Deceo, ui, ĕre, V N 2 Conj

Deceptio, ōnis N S 3 D f g

Decido, idi, ere, V N 3 Conj ex de & cado

Decipio, epi, ere, V A 3 Conj ex de & capio

Decor oris, N S 3 D m g

Decorus, a, um, N A 3 Term

Decurro, ri, ĕre, V N 3 Conj ex de & curro

Decus, ōris, N S 3 D n g

Deditus, a, um, Part Præt a dedor

Deduco, xi, ĕre, V A 3 Conj ex de & duco

Demior, tus fum uci, V P 3 Conj.

Defectio, ōnis, N S 3 D f g

Defectus, ûs N S 4 D m g.

Defero,

(133)

Defero, tuli, ferre, V A 3 Conj. ex de & fero.

Deficio, eci, ere, V A. 3 Conj ex de & facio

Deglutio, ivi, ire. V A 4 Conj

Delatio, onis, N S 3 D f g

Delector, atus sum, ri, V P 1 Conj.

Delicia, arum, N S 1 D f g

Demens, tis, N A 3 Art

Dementia, æ N S 1 D f g

Demissio, onis, N S 3 D f g

Demitto, si, ere V A 3 Conj. ex de & mitto.

Dens, tis, N S 3 D m g

Depressus, a, um, Part. Præt a Deprimor

Deprimo, si, ere, V A 3 Conj. ex de & primo

Derelinquens, tis, Part Præf a derelinqu)

Derelinquo, liqui, ere, V A 3 Conj ex de-re &
    linquo

Derideo, si, ere, V A 2 Conj ex de & rideo.

Derisor, oris, N S. 3 D m g.

Defero, ui, ere, V A 3 Conj. ex de & fero.

Defertum i, N S 2 D n g

Desideratissimus, a, um, N A 3 Term.

Desiderium, N S 2 D n g

Desidero, avi, are, V A 1 Conj

Desino, ivi, & ii, ere, V N 3 Conj

Desisto, stiti, ere, V A 3 Conj. ex de & sisto.

Despicior, ctus sum, ici, V P 3 Conj

Destituo, ui, ere, V A 3 Conj. ex de & statuo

Destruo, xi, ere, V A 3 Conj ex de & struo

Destruor, ctus sum, ui, V P 3 Conj

Desum, fui, esse, V. N Comp. ex de & sum

Detestor, atus sum, ari, V D 1 Conj ex de &
    testor

Detrunco, avi, are, V A. 1 Conj. ex de &
    trunco

Devasto, avi, are, V A. 1 Conj. ex de & vasto

Devenio, veni, ire, V N 4 Conj ex de & ve-
    nio.

H   Devolvo,

Devolvo, vi, ĕre, V A 3 Conj ex de & volvo

Deus, i, N S 2 D m g

Dico, xi, ĕre, V A 3 Conj

Dictus, i, um, Part Præt a dicor

Dies, ei N S 5 D f g

Dictum, i, N S 2 D n g

Difficlior, ōris N A 3 Art Com

Dignitas, tatis, N S 3 D f g

Dignus, a, um, N A 3 Term

Digredior, ssus sum di V D 3 Conj ex di & gradior

Dilectio ōnis, N S 3 D f g

Dilectus, a, um, Part Præt a diligor.

Diligens, tis, Part Præf

Diligo, xi, ĕre, V A 3 Conj ex di & lego

Dimitto, si, ĕre, V A 3 Conj ex di & mitto

Diminuor, utus sum, ui V P 3 Conj ex di & minuo

Dimoveor, otus sum, eri, V P 3 Conj ex di & moveor.

Dirigo rexi, regere, V A 4 Conj ex di & rego.

Dirimo, ēmi, ĕre V A 3 Conj ex dis & emo

Diruo, ŭi, ĕre, V A 3 Conj. ex di & ruo

Disco, didici, ĕre V A 3 Conj

Discursans, tis, Part Præf 3 Art.

Disjungo, xi, ĕre, V A 3 Conj ex dis & jungo

Disjungor, ctus sum, gi, V P 3 Conj ex dis & jungor

Dispello, ŭli, ĕre, V A 3 Conj ex dis & pello

Disciplina, æ N S 1 D f g

Disperdens, tis, Part Præf a disperdo.

Dispergo, si, ĕre, V A. 3 Conj ex di & spargo.

Disruptus, a, um, Part Præt a disrumpor.

Disseco, ŭi, āre, V A 1 Conj ex dis & seco

Ditesco, ĕre, V Inc 3 Conj

Dito, āvi, āre, V A 1 Conj

Ditor, ātus sum, āri, V P 1 Conj

Divarico, avi, are V A 1 Conj ex di & varico

Diversus, a um, N A 3 Term

Divus, ītis, N. A 3 Art.

Divinus.

Divinus, a, um, N A 3 Term
Divitiæ, arum, N. S 1 D. f g
D , dědi, āre, V A 1 Con,
Duceo, ŭi, ēic V. A 2 Conj
Doctrina, æ, N S 1 D f g
Dico, m, ēre, V N 2 Conj
Dolor, ōris, N S 3 D m g
Dolosus, a, um, N A 3 Fom
Dolus, i, N S 2 D. m g
Domina, æ N S 1 D f g
Dominans, tis, Put Præf dominor
Dominatio, ōnis, N S 3 D f g
Dominator, ōris, N S 3 D m. g
Dominor, ātus fum, ari, V D 1 Conj.
Dominus, i, N S 2 D m g
Domus, i, ûs, N S 2 & 4 D f g.
Donum, i, N S 2 D n g
Dormio, īvi, īre, V N. 4 Conj
Dormitatio, onis, N S 3 D f g
Dormito, āvi, āre, V N 1 Conj
Duco, xi, ěre, V A 3 Conj
Dulcedo, ĭnis, N S 3 D f. g.
Dulcis, is, N A 3 Art
Duo, orum, arum, orum, N A 3 Term.
Duro, āvi, āre, V A 1 Conj.
Durus, a, um, N A 3 Term.

E

Ebibo, bi, ěre, V A 3 Conj. ex e & bibo.
Ebrius, a, um, N A 3 Term
ecquis, ecqua, ecquid vel ecquid, Pron Interr.
Edo, ēdi, ere vel efle, V Irr 3 Conj
educo, xi, ěre, V A. 3 Conj. ab e & duco
Effectus, i um, Part Præt ab efficior
Effero, extuli, effene, V A 3 Conj ab ex &
to o

Efficior,

Efferor, elatus fum, efferri, V. P 3 Conj ab ex
   & feror

Efficio, ēci, ēie, V A 3 Conj ab ex & facio.

Efficior, eũus fum, ĩci, V P. 3 Conj ab ex & facior

Efflo, āvi, āre, V A 1 Conj ab ex & flo

Efflo efco, ĩ, ēie V Incep. 3 Conj

Effodio, ōdi, ēre, V. A 3 Conj ab ex & fodio

Effundens, tis Part Praef ab effundo

Egens, tis, Part Praet ab egeo

Egeo, ũi, ēre, V N 2 Conj

Egeftas, atis N S 3 D t g

Egredior, fius fum, di, V D 2 Conj ab e & gra.

Egreffus, us, N S 4 D m g   ferior

Ejicio, jeci, ēre, V A 3 Conj ab e & jacio

Elatio onis, N S 3 D f g

Elatus, a, um, Part Praet ab efferor

Eligo, ēgi, ēre, V A 3 Conj ab e & lego

Eloquor cutus fum, ōqui, V D. 3 Conj ab e &
   loquor

Emitto, fi, ēre, V A 3 Conj ab e & mitto.

Emolumentum i, N S. 2 D u g

Emptor, oris N S 3 D m g

Eo, ivi, ire, V N 4 Conj

Equus i, N S 2 D m g

Eripio, ui, ēre, V A 3 Conj ab e & rapio

Eripior, eptus fum, ip, V P 3 Conj ab e &
   rapior

Erigor, ectus fum, igi, V P. 3 Conj ab e & regor.

Ero, āvi, āre, V N 1 Conj

Error, ōris N S 3 D m g

Eructans, tis, Part praef ab Eructo.

Eructo, āvi, āre, V N. 1 Conj

Erudio, ivi, ire, V A 4 Conj

Eruditio, ōnis, N S. 3 D f g.

Efurio, ivi, ire, V N 4 Conj

Evado, fi, ere, V N 3 Conj ab e & vado.

Evello, velli & vulfi, ēre, V A 3 Conj. ab e &
   vello   Evellor,

Evellor, vulfus fum, velli, V P 3 Conj ab e
& vellor

Evenio, eni, ire, V N 4 Conj ab e & venio

Eventus, ûs, N 4 D m g

Everrens, tis, Part Præf ab everro.

Evertor, fus fum, ti, V P 3 Conj ab e & ver-
tor

Everto, ti, ěre, V A 3 Conj ab e & verto

Evomo, ŭi, ěre, V A 3 Conj ab e & vomio.

Exalto, avi, āre, V A 1 Conj

Exaudio, ivi, ire, V A 4 Conj ab ex & audio

Exaudior, itus fum, iri V P 4 Conj ab ex &
audio

Excandecentia, æ N S 1 D f. g

Excandefco, ui ěre, V Inc 3 Conj ab exc a-
deo

Excellens tis Part Præf ab excello

Excellentia, æ N S 1 D f g

Excellentior, N 3 Art Comp

Excretum ti, N S 2 D n g

Excernor, cretus fum, ni, V P 3 Conj ab ex &
cernor

Exco vi re, V A 1 Conj

Exgatio, ōnis, N S 3 D f g.

Excogito, avi, ire, V A 1 Conj ab ex & cogito

Excretio, ōnis N S 3 D f g

Excretu, rtus fum, āri, V D 1 Conj

Exeo ivi, ire, V N 4 Con, ab ex & eo

Exceo, ui, ěre, V A 2 Con, ab ex & uiceo

Excedor fus fum, ěri, V P 2 Conj ab ex &
ercer

Exhibeor, tus fum, ēri, V P 2 Conj ab ex
& habeor

Eximius, i, um, N A 3 Tcim

Exilio, exfilii, ěre V. N. 3 Conj ab ex & filio

Libror, atus sum āri, V P 1 Conj ab ex &
 cor

ʼ ofes um, N A 3 Term
Expetr o on, N S 3 D f g
L cth z āre, V A 1 Conj ab e & f, &,
L pendo d ēre V A 3 Conj au ex & penao.
Luperior, e.us sum īri, V D 3 Conj
L cior, ātus sum, āri, V P 1 Conj ab ex &
 cor

C len, t., ēre, V A 2 Conj ab e, & plen
I ficon, ā , ā V A 1 Conj ab ex & ficc
S rgeor, t.us sum, gui, V P 3 Conj ab e,
 & t.nea r

Lripto ā , āre, V A 1 Conj ab ex & ft po,
  o c, tih, ē e V A 3 Conj ab ex & tollo
I ætu r o um, N A 3 Term
  trem tas ā s N S 3 D f g
Ih o, ā, , āre, V N 1 Conj ab ex & falto
Lurgo g, ēre, V. N 3 Conj ab ex & turgo

F

FAlucans tic Part. Praef a fabrico
Fi e, e, N S 5 D f g
F co cc tre V V 3 Conj
Facul as atis N S 3 D f g
F ix, ācis, N A 3 Arc
  liras ātis, N S 3 D. f g
Fal ds, , um, N A 3 Term
I   æ, N S 1 D f g.
F me cus um, N A 3 Term
F n a a, N S 1 D f g
I tus is N S 1 D m g
F on f fusium un V D 2 Conj
I t a o, tis N S 3 D f g
F rgo, avi āre, V A 1 Conj
Ea us, , um, N A 3 Term.

Fator, ōris, N S 3 D m. g.

Fatus, i, N S 2 D m g

Fax, cis, N S 3 D f g

Ferio, percussi, īre V. A 4 Conj

Ferrum, i, N S 2 D n g

Fessus, a, um, Part Præl. a fatiscor

Festino, āvi, āre V A 1 Conj

Ficus, ûs, N S 4 D f g

Fidelis, is, N A. 3 Art

Fides, ei, N S. 5 D f g

Filucra, æ, N S 1 D f g

Filius, i, um, N A 3 Term.

Figo, x, ĕ e, V A. 3 Conj.

Filius, ii, N S 2 D m g

Filum, i, N S 2 D n. g

Findo, idi, ĕre, V A. 3 Conj.

Fingo, xi, ĕre, V A 3 Conj.

Finis, is, N S 3 D c g

Fio, factus sum, fieri, V N.

Firmitas, atis, N S 3 D f g.

Flagellum, i, N S. 2 D n g

Fleo, ēvi, ēre, V A 2 Conj.

Floreo, ui, ēre, V. N 2 Conj.

Fluentum, i, N S 2 D n g.

Fluo, xi, ĕre, V A 3 Conj.

Flumina, æ, N S 1 D f g.

Fœnus, ōris, N S 3 D n g.

Fœtidus a, um, N A 3 Term.

Fulgor, ōris, N S 3 D m g.

Fons, tis, N S 3 D m g.

Formica æ, N. S 1 D f g.

Formo, āvi, āre, V A 1 Conj.

Formor, atus sum, āri, V P. 1 Conj.

Fossa, æ N S 1 D f g

Fovea, æ, N S 1 D f g.

Foetor, tis, N S 3 D m g

Fractura, æ, N S 1 D f g.

Fractus,

Fractus, a, um, Part Præt a frangor.
Frango, ēgi, ĕe V A 3 Conj.
Frangor, fractus fum gi, V P 3 Conj
Fraudulentus, a, um N A 3 Term
Frigidus a, um, N A 3 Term
Frigus, ŏris, N S 3 D n g
Frænum i, N S 2 D r g
Fructus, ûs, N S 4 D m g
Fruor ctus vel itus, fiui, V D. 3 Conj
Fruſtum, i, N S 2 D n g
Fugo, āvi, āre, V A 1 Conj
Fugio gi, ĕre, V A 3 Conj
Fumus i, N S 2 D m g
Fundamentum, i, N S 2 D n g
Funis, is, N S 3 D m g
Fur is N S 3 D c g
Furibundus, a um N A 3 Term
Furibundus i, N. S 2 D m g
Furor ōris N S 3 D m g
Furor atus fum, ari V D. 1 Conj
Furtivus a um, N A 3 Term
Futorius, a um N A 3 Term
Futurus, a um a 1 um

G

Garrulus, a, um, N A 3 Term
Gemma æ, N S 1 D t g
Generatio ōnis N S 3 D t g
Genetrix, icis, N S 3 D t g
Gens tis N S 3 D t g
Gero ſi, ĕre, V A 3 Conj
Gigno, gĕnui, ĕre, V A 3 Conj
Gladius, ii, N S 2 D m g.
Gloria æ, N S. 1 D t g
Glorior, ātus fum, āri, V D. 1 Conj.
Gratia æ, N S 1 D t g.

Gratiofus,

Gratiofus, a, um, N A 3 Term.
Gratiffimus, a, um, N A 3 Term fuperl.
Gratus a, um, N A 3 Term.
Gravidus, a, um, N A 3 Term
Gravior, ōris, N A 3 Ait Comp
Gravis, is, N A 3 Ait
Grnnium, ii, N S 2 D n. g.
Greffus, fis, N S. 4 D m g

H.

HAbeo, üi, ēre, V A 2 Conj
Habeor, itus fum, ēii, V P 2 Conj.
Habito, āvi, āre, V A 1 Conj
Habitaculum, 1, N S 2 D n g.
Hereo, fi, ēre, V N. 2 Conj
Haurio, fi, īre, V A 4 Conj.
Herba, æ, N S 1 D f. g
He, hæc, hoc, Art
Hirundo, ïnis, N S 3 D f g.
Homo, ïnis, N S 3 D c g
Honor, ōris, N S. 3 D m g
Honorificus, a, um N A 3 Term.
Honoro, āvi, āre, V A. 1 Conj
Honoror, atus fum, āii, V P 1 Conj.
Humanus, a, um, N A 3 Term
Humilitas, ātis, N S 3 D f g
Hiems, ēmis, N S 3 D f g
Hypocrita, æ, N S 1 D m g

I.

JActo, avi, āre, V A 1 Conj.
Jaculor, ātus fum, āii, V D. 1 Conj
Jacto, æ, N S 1 D f g
Idem, eadem, idem, N A 3 Term.
Jehova, æ, N S 1 D m g

Igneus,

Ignavus a, um, N A. 3 Term.

Ignis is N S. 3 D m g

Ignominia, æ N S 3 D f g

Ignoro, a i, are, V A 1 Conj ab in & nosco

Illoqueor, ātus sum, āri, V. P 1 Conj ab in & loquecr

Ille illa, illud, Pron

Illudo, li, ěre, V A. 3 Conj ab in & ludo

Illumino, āvi, āre, V A. 1 Conj. ab in & lumino

Illustro, ā. , :re, V A 1 Conj. ab in & lustro.

Immeritus, a, um, N A 3 Term

Immisceo, cui, ěre, V. A. 2 Conj. ab in & misceo

Immitto, si, ěre, V A. 3 Conj. ab in & mitto.

Immoror, atus sum, ari, V D 1 Conj ab in & moror

Immundus, a, um, N A. 3 Term.

Imperium, ii, N S 2 D n g.

Impero, avi, are, V A 1 Conj ab in & paro.

Impietas, ātis, N S 3 D f g

Impingo, ēgi, ěre, V A 3 Conj ab in & pango

Impius, a, um, N A 3 Term

Impleor, ētus sum, ēri, V P 2 Conj. ab in & pleo

Impono, sui, ěre, V A 3 Conj ab in & pono.

Improbitas, ātis, N S 3 D f g.

Improbus, a, um, N A 3 Term

Improbus, i, N. S 2 D. m g.

Impulsu, a, um, Part Præt. ab impellor.

Impunis is, N A 3 Art

Impunitus, a, um, N A 3 Term

Imputor, atus sum, ari, V. P 1 Conj ab in & puor

Incantatio, ōnis, N S 3 D f g

Incedo, ssi, ěre, V. N 3 Conj ab in & cedo

Incid

Incido di, ĕre, V A 3 Conj ab in & cado

Inclino, āvi, are, V. A 1 Conj

Increpatio, ōnis, N S 3 D f g

Incumbo, cŭbui, ĕre, V. N 3 Conj ab in &
   cumbo

Incurvo, āvi, ue, V A 1 Conj ab in & curvo

Indigeo, ŭi, ere V. N 2 Conj

Indico, xi, ĕre, V A 3 Conj ex in & dico

Indignabundus, a, um, N A 3 Term

Indignatio, ōnis, N S 3 D f g

Indignor, ātus sum, ari, V. D 1 Conj ab in &
   dignor

Indigus, a, um, N A 3 Term

Indo, didi, ere, V A 3 Conj ab in & do

Induo, ŭi, ĕre, V A 3 Conj ab in & duo

Industrius, a, um, N A 3 Term

Inebrians, tis, Part Præf ab inebrio

Ineo, ivi, īre, V N 4 Conj ab in & eo

Infamia, æ, N. S 1 D f g

Infernus i, N S 2 D m g

Infero tŭli, ferre, V A Irreg ab in & fero

Ingredior, ssus sum, di, V D 3 Conj. ab in &
   gradior.

Injicio, ēci, ĕre, V. A 3 Conj ab in & jaceo

Inimicus, i, N S 2 D m g

Iniquitas, atis, N S 3 D f g

Iniquus, a, um, N A 3 Term

Initium, ii, N S 2 D n g

Injustus, a, um, N A 3 Term

Innitor, xus, vel sus sum, V D 3 Conj. ab in
   & nitor

Innocens, tis, N A 3 Art

Innotesco, ŭi, ĕre V Inc 3 Conj

Inopia, æ N S 1 D f g

Inquiro, sivi, ĕre, V A 3 Conj ab in & quæro.

Insaniens, tis Part Præf ab insanio

Insanus, a, um, N. A 3 Term

Inscrutabilis,

Inscrutabilis, is, N. A 3 Art

Insector, atus sum, ri, V D 1 Conj ab in &
 sector

Insilæ, arum, N S 1 D f g

Insidens, tis, Part Præf ab

Insideo, edi, ere, V N 2 Conj ab in & sedeo.

Insidior, tus sum, ari, V D 1 Conj.

Insignis, is, N A 3 Art

Inspectio, onis, N S 3 D f g

Instrumentum, i, N S 2 D n g

Instruo,   , ere, V A 3 Conj ab in & struo

Instructus, ctus sum, ui, V P 3 Conj ab in &
 struo

Insum, fui, esse, V N ab in & sum

Insurrectio, onis, N S 3 D f g

Integer, ra, rum, N A. 3 Term.

Integritas, atis, N S 3 D f g

Intellectus, us, N S 4 D m g

Intelligens, tis, Part Præf ab intelligo.

Intelligentia, æ, N S 1 D f g

Intelligo, xi, ere, V A 3 Conj ab inter & lego.

Interfector, oris, N S 3 D m g

Intermisceo, cui, cre, V A 2 Conj ab inter &
 misceo

Interpello, avi, are, V A 1 Conj ab inter &
 pello

Intueor, itus sum, eri, V D. 2 Conj ab in &
 tueor

Invenio, eni, ire, V. A 4 Conj. ab in & venio

Invenior, ventus sum, iri, V P 4 Conj. ab in
 & venior

Inversio, onis, N S. 3 D f g.

Investigo, avi, are, V. A 1 Conj ab in & vestigo

Invideo, di, ere, V A 2 Conj.

Invidia, æ, N S 1 D f g

Jocus, i, N. S 2 D pl. 1 & a

Ipfe, ipfa, ipfum, Pron.

Ira, æ, N S 1 D f g

Iracundus, a, um, N A. 3 Term.

Iracundus, i, N S 2 D m g.

Iratus, a, um, N. A 3 Term.

Irretior, ītus fum, iri, V P. 4 Conj. ab in &
    rete.

Irritus, a, um, N A. 3 Term. ab in & ratus.

Is, ea, id, Pron.

Ifte, ifta, iftud, Pron

Iter, īnĕris, N S. 3 D. n g

Judicium, ii, N S 2 D. n g

Judico, āvi, āre, V A 1 Conj. a judex.

Jumentum, i, N S 2 D. n g.

Juramentum, i, N. S, 2 D. n. g.

Jurgium, ii, N S 2 D n g

Juro, āvi, āre, V A 1 Conj.

Jus, ris, N S 3 D n g

Juftitia, æ, N S 1 D f g.

Juftus, a, um, N A 3 Term.

Juvenis, is, N S 3 D. c. g.

L.

Labium, ii, N S. 2 D. n. g.

Labor, ōris, N. S. 3 D m g.

Labor, lapfus fum, labi, V. D 3 Conj.

Laborans, tis, Part Præf a laboro.

Laboro, āvi, āre, V N. 1 Conj.

Lac, lactis, N S. 3 D n. g.

Lacero, āvi, āre, V. A. 1 Conj

Lætifico, āvi, āre, V. A. 1 Conj. ex lætus &
    facio.

Lætitia, æ, N. S. 1 D. f. g.

Lætor, atus fum, āri, V. D. 1 Conj.

Lætus, a, um, N. A. 3 Term.

Lanx, cis, N. S. 3 D. f. g.

I

Lapideu

Lapideus, a, um, N A 3 Term.
Lapis, ĭdis, N S 3 D. m g
Lapfus, ûs, N S 4 D m g.
Laqueus, i, N S 2 D m g
Largior, ītus fum, iri, V D 4 Conj
Latebiæ, arum, N S 1 D f g.
Latus, a, um, N. A. 3 Term
'Laudo, āvi, āre, V. A 1 Conj.
Laudor, ātus fum, āri, V P. 1 Conj.
Laus, dis, N. S 3 D f. g
Laxo, āvi, āre, V A 1 Conj
Lectio, ōnis, N S 3 D f g.
Lectiffimus, a, um, N A 3 Term.
Lectus, i, N S 2 D m g.
Legatus, i, N S. 2 D m g
Leo, ōnis, N S 3 D m. g.
Lethalis, is, N A 3 Art.
Lex, gis, N S 3 D. f g
Liber, ri, N S 2 D m g.
Liberi, orum, N S 2 D m. g
Libero, avi, are, V A 1 Conj
Liberor, ātus fum, āri, V.P 1 Conj
Lignum, i, N. S. 2 D n. g
Lingua, æ, N. S 1 D. f g.
Lis, litis, N S 3 D f. g
Litigium, ii, N. S 2 D n g.
Litigo, āvi, āre, V N. 1 Conj a lites & agu.
Loculus, i, N S 2 D m g
Locus, i, N. S. 2 D m g
Longanimis, is, N A. 3 Art.
Longanimitas, tatis, N S. 3 D f g.
Longinquus, a, um, N A 3 Term.
Loquacitas, ātis, N. S 3 D f g.
Loquax, acis, N. A. 3 Art.
Loquens, tis, Part. Præf. a loquor.
Loquor, cutus fum, loqui, V D 3 Conj.
Luceo, luxi, ēre, V. N. 2 Conj

Lucerna, æ, N. S. 1 D. f. g.
Lucrum, i, N S. 2 D. n. g
Luctus, ûs, N S 4 D. m g
Ludo, fi, ĕre, V A 3 Conj
Ludus, i, N S 2 D. m g
Lumen, īnis N S 3 D. n g
Lux, lucis, N S. 3 D f g
Luxatus, a, um, N. A 3 Term.

M.

M Aceria, æ, N. S 1 D f g
Machinatio, ōnis, N S 3 D. f g
Magnates, um, N. S 3 D. m g.
Magnus, a, um, N A 3 Term.
Major, oris, N A. 3 Art. Comp. ex magnus.
Majores, um, N S. 3 D m. g.
Maledico, xi, ĕre, V. A. 3 Conj. ex male &
    dico
Maledictio, ōnis, N S 3 D f g
Maleficus, a, um, N. A. 3 Term.
Malignus, a, um, N A 3 Term
Malitia, æ, N. S 1 D. f. g
Malum, i, N S 2 D n. g
Malus, a, um, N. A. 3 Term.
Maneo, fi, ēre, V. N 2 Conj
Manifeftus, a, um, N A. 3 Term.
Manfuetus, a, um, N. A 3 Term.
Manus, ûs, N. S. 4 D f g.
Marculus, i, N S. 2 D. m g.
Maritus, i, N S. 2 D m g
Mater, tris, N. S 3 D. f g
Medicina, æ, N S 1 D f g
Meditans, tis, Part. Præf. a meditor
Meditor, atus fum, āri, V D. 1 Conj.
Medium, ii, N S 2 D n g.
Mel, mellis, N. S. 3 D n g.

Melior,

Melior, ōris, N A Comp a bonus, 3 Art
Memoria, æ N S 1 D f g
Mendax, ācis, N S 3 Art.
Mendacium, ii, N S 2 D n g
Mendico, avi, āre, V N 1 Conj.
Mensura, æ, N S 1 D f. g
Mentiens, tis, Part Præf. a mentior
Mentior, titus sum, iri, V D 4 Conj.
Merces ēdis, N S 3 D f g
Meridies, ei, N S. 5 D f g.
Meffis, is N S 3 D. f g
Meto, meffui, ēre, V A 3 Conj
Metus, ûs, N S 4 D m g
Minister, tri, N S 2 D m g
Miror, ātus sum, āri, V D 1 Conj
Mifceo, ui, ēre, V A. 2 Conj
Miferatio, ōnis, N S 3 D f g.
Miferia, æ N. S 1 D f. g
Mifericordia, æ, N S. 1 D f g.
Miffio, ōnis, N S 3 D f g
Mittens, tis, Part Præf a mitto
Mittor, miffus sum, mitti, V P. 3 Conj
Mixtus, a, um, Part. Præt a mifceor
Moderor, ātus sum, ari, V D 1 Conj
Modeftus, a, um, N A. 3 Term
Mœror, ōris, N S. 3 D m g
Mæftitia, æ, N. S. 1 D f g.
Molaris, is, N. S 3 D m g
Moleftia, æ N S 1 D f g
Moleftus, a, um, N A 3 Term.
Molilio, īvi, īre, V A 4 Conj
Mollis is, N A 3 Art
Momentum. i, N S. 2 D n g
Monile, is N S. 3 D n g
Mordeo, momordi, ēre, V. A 2 Conj
Morior, mortuus sum, mori, V D 3 Conj.
Moror, atus sum, āri, V. D. 1 Conj.

Mors.

Mors, tis, N S 3 D f g.

Mortarium, ii, N S. 2 D n. g.

Mortuus, a, um, N. A. 3 Term.

Mulcto, āvi, āre, V A. 1 Conj

Mulctor, ātus sum, āri, V P 1 Conj.

Mulier, ĕris, N. S 3 D f. g

Multiplico, āvi, āre, V A 1 Conj a multiplex.

Multiplicor, atus sum. āri, V P. 1 Conj.

Multitudo, ĭnis, N S. 3 D f. g.

Multus, a, um, N A 3 Term.

Mundities, ei, N S 5 D. f g.

Mundus, a, um, N. A. 3 Term

Munitus, a, um, Par. Præt. a munior.

Munus, eris, N S 3 D. n g.

Murus, i, N. S. 2 D m g.

Musca, æ N. S. 1 D. f g

Mutatio, ōnis, N S 3 D f g

Mutor, atus sum, āri, V. P 1 Conj

Mutuans, tis, Part. Præs a mutuo.

Mutus, a, um, N A 3 Term

N.

NAscor, natus sum, nasci, V D. 3 Conj.
Nasus, i, N S 2 D m. g.

Natio, onis, N S. 3 D f g

Nativitas, atis, N S. 3 D f g

Nemo, inis, N. S 3 D c. g

Nequam, N. A. Indecl.

Nescio, īvi, īre. V N. 4 Conj. ex ne & scio.

Nicto, āre, V. N 1 Conj.

Nidus, i, N. S. 2 D m g

Niger, gra. grum, N. A 3 Term.

Nihil, N Indec. a nihilum.

Nitidus, a, um, N. A 3 Term.

Nitrum, i, N S. 2 D n g.

Nivalis, is, N. A. 3 Art

Nix,

Nix, nivis, N S 3 D f g
Nolo, ui, lle V Irr
Nomen, ĭnis, N S 3 D n g
Nosco, ōvi, ĕre, V A 3 Conj
Novus, a, um, N A 3 Term
Nubes, is, N S 3 D f g.
Nudus, a, um, N. A. 3 Term
Nullus, a, um, N A. 3 Term.
Numeror, atus sum, ari, V P 1 Conj.
Nuntius, i, N. S 2 D. m g

O

OBductus, a, um, Part Præt ab obducor
Obduro, āvi, āre, V N 1 Conj ex ob &
duro
Obedio, īvi, īe, V N 4 Conj ex ob & audio
Oberro, āvi, āre, V A 1 Conj ex ob & erro
Obfirmo, āvi, āre, V A 1 Conj ex ob & firmo.
Oblectatio, ōnis, N S. 3 D f g.
Obscurus a, um, N A 3 Term
Observo, āvi, āre, V A 1 Conj ex ob & servo
Observor, atus sum, V P 1 Conj ex ob & servor.
Obsisto, stĭti, ĕre, V N 3 Conj ex ob & sisto.
Obtego, xi ĕre, V A. 3 Conj ex ob & tego
Obtineo, ui, ēre, V A 2 Conj ex ob & teneo.
Obtrectans, tis, Part Præs ab obtrecto.
Obturo, āvi, āre, V A 1 Conj ex ob & turo
Obvenio ēni, īre, V N 4 Conj ex ob & venio?
Occasio, ōnis N S 3 D f g
Occido, di, ĕre, V A 3 Conj ex ob & cædo
Occlusus, a um, Part Præt ab occludor.
Occulto, āvi, āre, V A 1 Conj
Occultor, atus sum ari, V P 1 Conj.
Occultus, a, um, N A 3 Term
Occupatio, ōnis, N S 3 D f g.
Occurro, ri ĕre, V N. 3 Conj ex ob & curro.
Oculus, i, N S. 2 D. m. g.   Odi,

Odi, V Def. ab odio

Odium, i, N. S 2 D n g

Offendo, di, ěre, V A 3 Conj.

Offendor, ius fum, di, V. P. 3 Conj

Offero, obtuli, offerre, V. A 3 Conj ex ob & f-ro

Officium ii, N S 2 D n. g

Oleum, i, N. S 2 D n g.

Olla, æ, N S 1 D f g

Olus, ěris, N S 3 D n g.

Omnis, e, N A 3 Art

Operarius, ii, N. S. 2 D m g

Operor, ātus fum, āri, V. D 1 Conj

Opes, um, N S. 3 D f g.

Oportet, V. Imp 2 Conj.

Oppreſſio, ōnis, N. S 3 D. f g.

Oppreſſor, ōris, N S 3 D m g.

Opprimens, tis, Part. Præf. ab opprimo

Opprimo, ſſi, ěre, V A. 3 Conj ex ob & premo.

Opprimor, ſſus fum, ïmi, V. P. 3 Conj ex ob & premor.

Opratior, ōris, N. A 3 Art. Comp

Opus, ěris, N S 3 D. n g

Oratio, ōnis, N S. 3 D f g

Orbatus, a, um, Part Præt ab orbor.

Orbita, æ, N S. 1 D f g.

Ornamentum, i, N S 2 D. n. g.

Ornatus, ûs, N S 4 D m g.

Os, ōris, N. S 3 D n g.

Os, oſſis, N S. 3 D. n g.

Oſculor, ātus fum, ari, V D. 1 Conj.

Oſculum, i, N. S. 2 D. n. g.

P.

PAlatum, i, N. S 2 D n g

Palpebra, æ N. S. 1 D f g.

Pando, di, ěre, V. A 3 Conj   Pandor,

Pandor, fus fum, di, V P 3 Conj.
Panis, is, N. S 3 D m. g
Panniculus, i, N. S. 2 D m g.
Parco, peperci, ĕre, V. N. 3 Conj.
Pario, peperi, ĕre, V. A. 3 Conj
Paror, atus fum, āri, V. P. 1 Conj.
Pars, tis, N. S 3 D. f. g
Partior, ītus fum, iri. V D 4 Conj.
Parvus, a, um, N A 3 Term.
Pafco, pāvi, ĕre, V A 3 Conj
Pafcor, paftus fum, fci, V P. 3 Conj.
Pater, tris, N S 3 D m. g
Paternus, a, um, N A 3 Term
Pauculus, a, um, N A. 3 Term.
Paucus, a, um, N A 3 Term.
Paveo, vi, ēre, V N 2 Conj.
Pavor, ōris, N S 3 D. m g.
Pauper, ĕris, N A. 3 Art.
Paupertas, atis, N S 3 D f g.
Pax, pacis N. S 3 D f g
Peccator, ōris, N S 3 D m g.
Peccatum, i, N. S 2 D. n. g
Pecco, avi, āre, V. N. 1 Conj
Pecunia, æ, N S. 1 D. f. g.
Pelliceo, xi, ĕre, V A. 3 Conj ex per & lacio.
Penetrale is, N S 3 D n g.
Peragor, actus, fum, āgi, V P. 3 Conj. ex per & agor.
Percipio, ēpi, ĕre, V A 3 Conj. ex per & capio.
Percutio, ffi, ĕre, V A 3 Conj. ex per & quatio.
Perditio, ōnis, N S 3 D f g
Perdo didi, ĕre, V. A 3 Conj ex per & do.
Perdor, ītus fum, V P 3 Conj.
Pereo, īvi, ii, īre, V. N 4 Conj ex per & eo
Perfectus, a, um, Part Præt a perficior
Perfero tūli, ferre V A 3 Conj ex per & fero.
Perficio, ēci, ĕre, V A 3 Conj ex per & facio.
Perfidiofus, a, um, N. A. 3 Term.

Perfidus,

Perfidus, a, um, N. A 3 Term

Periclitor, atus sum, ari, V. D. 1 Conj

Peritus, a, um, N A. 3 Term

Permissus, a, um, Part Præt a permittor.

Permitto, si, ĕre, V A 3 Conj ex per & mitto.

Perparvus, a, um, N A 3 Term

Perpendo, di ĕre, V. A 3 Conj. ex per & pendo.

Perpetro, āvi, āre, V A 1 Conj ex per & patro.

Perpetuus, a, um, N. A 3 Term

Perrumpo, upi, ĕre, V A 3 Conj ex per & rumpo

Persequens, tis, Part Præt a Persequor

Persequor, cutus sum, qui V D. 3 Conj. ex per & sequor

Persina, æ, N S 1 D. f. g

Perstillo, āvi, āre, V N 1 Conj ex per & stillo.

Perturbatio, ōnis, N S 3 D f g

Perturbor, ātus sum, āri, V P. 1 Conj ex per & turbor.

Pervenio, vēni, īre, V. N. 4 Conj ex per & venio

Perversitas, ātis, N S 3 D f g

Perversus, a, um, Part Præt a pervertor

Perverto, ti, ĕre, V A 3 Conj ex per & verto.

Pervestigans, tis, Part Præs a pervestigo

Pervestigo, āvi, are, V A 1 Conj. ex per & vestigo

Pes, pedis, N S 3 D m g

Pessimus, i, um, Sup a malus

Pharmacopola æ, N S. 1 D m g.

Piger, ra, rum, N A 3 Term

Pignus, ŏris, N. S 3 D n g

Pigritia, æ, N S 1 D F g

Pinguefacio, ēci, ĕre, V A 3 Conj ex pinguis & facio

Pinguis, is, N A 3 Art.

Pistillum, i, N S 2 D n g

Plaga, æ, N. S. 1 D f. g.

Plango

Plango, xi, ĕre, V A. 3 Conj

Plantatus, a, um, Part Præt. a Plantor.

Planto, āvi, are, V A. 1 Conj.

Planus, a, um, N A 3 Term.

Platea, æ, N S 1 D f g

Plenus, a um, N A. 3 Term.

Plurimius, a, um, N A 3 Term.

Pluvia, æ, N S 1 D f g

Pœna, æ, N S 1 D f g

Ponderosus, a, um, N A 3 Term.

Pondus, ĕris, N S 3 D n. g.

Pono, sui, ere V A 3 Conj

Ponor, situs sum, ni, V. P 3 Conj.

Populus, i, N. S 2 D m g

Porcus, i N. S. 2 D m. g.

Porta, æ, N S. 1 D f g

Possessio, ōnis, N S 3 D f. g.

Possessor, ōris, N. S 3 D. m g.

Possidens, tis, Part. Præs. a Possideo.

Possideo, ēdi, ēre, V A 2 Conj ex potis & sedeo.

Possum, potui, posse, V N.

Potens, tis, Part a possum.

Potestas, ātis, N. S 3 D f g.

Potus, us, N. S. 4 D m g

Præbeo, ŭi, ēre, V A 2 Conj ex præ & habeo.

Præceps, ĭtis, N A 3 Art.

Præceptum, i, N S 2 D n g

Præcipito, avi, are, V. A 1 Conj

Præcipuus. a, um, N A 3 Term

Prædico, xi, ere, V A 3 Conj ex præ & dico.

Præditus, a, um, N A. 3 Term

Prælium, ii, N S. 2 D n. g

Præparatio, onis, N S 3 D. f g

Præsepe, is, N. S. 3 D. n g.

Prætereo, īvi, īre, V A. 4 Conj. ex præter & eo

Prævaricor, atus sum, āri, V D 1 Conj.

Prævideo, di, ēre, V. A ex præ & video.

Precor

Precor, atus fum, ari, V D 1 Conj

Prehendo, di, ere, V A 3 Conj.

Preſſura, æ, N. S 1 D. f. g.

Pretioſus, a, um, N. A 3 Term.

Pretium, ii, N. S 2 D n g

Primitiæ, arum N. S 1 D f. g.

Primus, a, um. N. A 3 Term. ſuperl a Pridem

Princeps, ipis, N S. 3 D c g

Principium, ii, N S 2 D n g

Prior, ōris, N A 3 Art. Comp. a Pridem

Probo, āvi, āre, V. A 1 Conj

Probrum, i, N. S. 2 D n. g

Probus, a, um, N A. 3 Term.

Procedo, ſſi, ĕre, V. N 3 Conj ex pro & cedo.

Proclamo, avi, āre, V. A 1 Conj ex pro & clamo

Prodeo, īvi, vel ii, īre, V N. 4 Conj ex pro & eo

Prodo, dĭdi, ĕre, V A 3 Conj ex pro & do.

Profero, tŭli, ferre, V A 3 Conj. ex pro & fero.

Profunditas, ātis N S. 3 D f g

Profundus, a, um, N A 3 Term.

Projicio, ēci, ĕre, V A 3 Conj ex pro & jaceo.

Prolatus, a, um, Part Præt a Proferor.

Prolongo, āvi, āre, V. A 1 Conj

Prenuncio, āvi, are, V A 1 Conj. ex pro & nuncio

Propero, āvi, āre, V. A 1 Conj

Propinquus, a, um, N A 3 Term

Propoſitum. i, N S 2 D n g

Prorogor, ātus fum, āri, V. P. 1 Conj ex pro & rogor

Proſpero, āvi, are, V A 1 Conj.

Proſum, fui, prodeſſe, V N ex pro & ſum.

Protractus, a, um, Part Præt a protrahor.

Proventus, us, N S 4 D m g.

Provincia, æ, N S 1 D f g.

Provocatus,

Provocatus, a, um, Part. Præt. a Provocor.
Proximus, i, N S 2 D. m g.
Prudens, tis, N A 3 Art.
Prudentia, æ, N. S. 1 D f g
Pruna, æ, N S 1 D f. g.
Pudefaciens, tis, Part Præf a pudefacio.
Pudefacio, ēci, ĕre, V A 3 Conj.
Puer i, N S 2 D. m g.
Pueritia, æ, N S 1 D. f. g.
Pulcher, ra, rum, N A. 3 Term
Pulchritudo, inis, N S. 3 D f g
Purifico, āvi, āre, V. A. 1 Conj ex purus &
   facio
Purus, a, um, N A 3 Term.
Puteus, i, N S 2 D m g
Putredo, ĭnis, N S 3 D f g.
Putrefco, V. Inc 3 Conj.

Q

QUærens, tis, Part Præf a quæro
   Quæro, fivi, ĕre, V. A 3 Conj.
Quæsitus, ûs, N S 4 D m g.
Quatuor N A Indecl
Qui, quæ, quod, Pron Relat.
Quies, tis, N S. 3 D f. g
Quiesco, ēvi, ĕre, V. Incept 3 Conj.
Quis, Quæ, Quid vel Quod, Pron.
Quisquam, quæquam, quidquam, Pron Comp.
Quisque, Quæque, Quidque vel Quodque, Pron
   Comp.
Quisquis, quicquid, Pron Comp.
Quivis, Quævis, Quodvis, Pron. Comp.

R

Radix, icis, N S 3 D f g

Ramus, 1, N S 2 D m g.

Ratio, ōnis, N S 3 D f. g

Ratiocinium, ii, N S 2 D n g

Rebellio, ōnis, N S 3 D f g.

Recedo, sli, ĕre, V N 3 Conj ex re & cedo.

Receptus, a, um, Part Præt a recipior

Recipio, cpi, ere, V A 3 Conj ex re & capio

Recondor, itus sum, di, V P 3 Conj ex re &
condor

Rector, ōris, N S 3 D. m. g.

Rectum, 1, N S 2 D n g

Rectus, a, um, N A. 3 Term

Recusans, tis Part Præs a recuso.

Redemptio, ōnis, N S. 3 D f g

Reddo, dĭdi, ĕre, V A 3 Conj ex re & do.

Reddor, ĭtus sum, di, V. P 3 Conj

Redeo, ivi, ire, V N 4 Conj ex re & eo

Reduco, xi, ĕre, V A. 3 Conj ex re & duco.

Regio, ōnis, N S. 3 D. f g.

Relinquo, iqui, ere, V. A 3 Conj ex re & lin-
quo

Remissus, a, nm, Part Præt a remittor

Remitto, si, ere, V A 3 Conj ex re & mitto

Removeo, vi, ēre, V A 2 Conj ex re & moveo

Remuneror, atus sum, āri, V. P 1 Conj. ex re &
muneror.

Renovo, ivi, āre, V A 1 Conj ex re & novo.

Renuo, ui, ĕre, V N. 3 Conj ex re & nuo

Rependo, di, ĕre, V. A. 3 Conj ex re & pendo.

Rependor, sus sum, di, V P. 3 onj ex re &
pendor.

K   Rependimus,

Repentimus, a, um, N A 3 Term

Repletus, a, um, Part Pret a repleor

Repono, fui, ĕre, V A 3 Conj ex re & pono

Reporto, avi, āre, V A 1 Conj ex re & por-
to

Reprehensor, ōris N S 3 D m g

Repuror, a us fum, āri, V. P 1 Conj ex re &
puror

Requiesco, ēvi, ĕre, V Inc 3 Conj ex re &
quiesco

Res, ei, N S 5 D f g

Rescindor, cisus fum, di, V. P 3 Conj ex re &
scindor

Resipisco, ni, ĕre, V. N 3 Conj ex resipio,
quod ex re & sapi.

Respicio, xi, ĕre, V. A 3 Conj ex re & specio

Respondeo, di, ēre, V. N 2 Conj. ex re & spondeo

Responsio, onis, N S 3 D f g.

Responsum, i, N S 2 D n g

Respuo, ŭi, ĕre, V A 3 Conj ex re & spuo.

Restituo, ŭi, ĕre, V A 3 Conj ex re & statuo

Rete is, N S 3 D n g

Retego x, ĕre, V A 3 Conj ex re & tego

Retineo ui, ēre, V A 2 Conj ex re & teneo.

Retributio ōnis, N S 3 D f g

Retrogredior, gressus fum, grĕdi, V D 3 Conj
ex retro & gradior

Revelo, avi āre V. A 1 Conj. ex re & velo

Revelor, atus fum, āri, V. P 1 Conj ex re &
velor

Revereor, itus fum, ēri, V D 2 Conj ex re &
vereor

Reverentia, æ, N S 1 D f g.

Reverto, ti, ĕre, V. A. 3 Conj. ex re & verto.

Rous, i, um N A 3 Term.

Res, regs, N S 3 D m g

Rdon n, ere, V N 2 Conj

Rio, fu āre, V A Conj

Rogo, tus fum, āri, V P 1 Conj.

Res, tis N S 4 D m g

Potis, i, N S 2 D m g

Romar, ous, N S 3 D n g

Robusfimus, a, um, N A 3 Term Sup

Robustus, a, um, N A 3 Term

Robustus, i, N S 2 D m g

Rogo, avi, re, V A 1 Conj

Ro, ionis, N S 3 D m g

Rostrum, i, N S 2 D n g

Rota, æ, N S 1 D f g

Ruber, ra, rum, N A 3 Term

Rugiens, tis, Part Præf a rugio

Rigrus, ûs, N S 4 D m g

Rura, æ, N S 1 D f g

Rura, ru, æe, V N 3 Conj

S

Sacer, cra, crum, N A 3 Term

Sicrificans, tis, Part Præf a sacrifico

Sacrum, ii, N S 2 D n g.

Sacro, avi, are, V A 1 Conj ex Sacrum & facio

Scrum, i N S 2 D n g

Sagitatus a um, Part Præf a sagitto

Sig e, N S 1 D f g

Silo, avi, āre V A 1 Conj

Silus, utis, N S 3 D f g

Saluter, ra, rum, N A 3 Term.

Salus, a, um N A 3 Term.

Sanctus, a, um, N A 3 Term

Sanguinarius, a, um, N A 3 Term

Sanguis,

Segus, inis, N S 3 D m g.
sana, a, um, N A 3 Term
Sapiens, tis, tert Iræ a sapio.
Sapientia æ N S 3 D f g
Sao, ivi vel i, V N 3 Conj
sarietas ātis, N S 3 D f g
Sario, ātus sum ar, V P, Conj
Sartor, ōris, N A 3 Art Con. a saris
Sartu, ra, um, N A 3 Term
Saturitas, ātis, N S 3 D f g
Sartuor, atus sum, ri, V P, Conj
sca ango, Inis N S 3 D f g
sceleratus, a, um, N A 3 Term
Sceleus, ēris, N S 3 D m g
scientia, æ, N S 3 D. f g
scio ivi ire V A 4 Conj
scob a, æ, N S 3 D f g
scr am tis Iert Iral a scortor
Scirpus, N S 2 D. m g
Scaber, i, N S 2 D m g
Scutor ātis sum, ar, V D 1 Conj
scculum, i N S 2 D n g
sectuus, a, um, N A 3 Term
Securu a um N A 3 Term
seco, c, ēc V N 2 Conj
Seco, ai, cre, V A 1 Conj
Seduco, xi, ec, V A, 3 Conj ex se & duco,
Sedulus a, um, N A 3 Term
Segmen, inis, N S 3 D n g
semino ivi ā, V A 1 Conj a semen
Semita æ N S 3 D f g
Senesco, ui, ēre, V Inc 3 Conj a seneo.
Senex, is, N S 3 D c g
Sententia, æ, N S 3 D f g
Seres, is, N S, 3 D f g
Sepimertum i N S 2 D n g
Sepulcrum, i N. S. 3 D. n g

Sepultura,

Sepultura, æ, N S 1 D f g
Sciens, tis, Part Præf a fero
Serenum i, N S 2 D n g
Sermo, ōnis, N S 3 D m g
Sero, ui, ĕre, V A 3 Conj
Serotinus, a, um, N A 3 Term.
Serpens tis, N S 3 D c g
Servo, āvi, are V A 1 Conj
Servor, ātus fum, ari, V P. 1 Conj.
Servus, i, N S 2 D m g
Siccus, a, um, N A 3 Term.
Sicco, ŭi, ēre, V N 2 Conj
Similis, is, N. A. 3 Art
Simulo, āvi, āre, V A 1 Conj
Singulus, a, um, N A 3 Term.
Sino, vi, cre, V. A. 3 Conj
Sinus, ûs, N S. 4 D. m. g
Sitio, ivi, īre, V A 4 Conj.
Siccus, ii, N S 2 D m g
Sol, folis, N S 3 D m g.
Solertia, æ, N S 1 D f g
Sonus, a, um, N A 3 Tem.
Solium, ii, N S 2 D n g
Somnum, ii N S 2 D n g.
Somnus i N S. 2 D m g
Soror, ō is, N S 3 D m g.
Sordes is, N S 3 D f g.
Sors t s, N S 3 D f g
Soror, ōris, N S 3 D f g
Sparo, fi, cre, V A 3 Conj
Spargor, fus fum, gi, V P 3 Conj.
Specto, vi āre, V A 1 Conj
Speculans, tis, Part Præ. a fpeculor
Sperno, fprevi, ĕre, V A 3 Conj.
Spes, ei, N S 4 D f g
Spina, æ, N S. 1 D f g.
Spiritus, ûs, N S. 4 D. m. g.

K 3   Splendidus,

Splendidus a, um, N A 3 Term.
Spolio, āvi, are, V A 1 Conj.
Spolium, ii, N S 2 D n. g.
Spondeo, fpofpondi, dēre, V A 2 Conj.
Sponfio, ōnis, N S 3 D f g
Sponfor, oris N S 3 D m g
Stabilio, īvi, īre, V A 4 Conj
Stabilior, itus fum, īri, V P 4 Conj.
Statuo, ūi, ēre, V A 3 Conj.
Status, ûs, N S 4 D m. g.
Stilla, æ, N S 1 D f g
Sto, stēti, āre, V N 1 Conj
Stoliditas, atis, N. S. 3 D f g.
Stolidus, a, um, N A 3 Term
Strieperus, a, um, N A. 3 Term
Stultitia, æ, N S 1 D f g
Stultus, a, um, N A 3 Term.
Stultus, i, N S 2 D m. g
Suavis, is, N A 3 Art
Suavitas, atis, N S 3 D. f g.
Subjicio, ēci, ere, V A 3 Conj. ex fub & jaceo.
Submiffio, ōnis, N S 3 D f g
Submiffus, a. um Part. Præt a submittor.
Subfanno, āvi āre, V. A 1 Conj
Subftantia, æ, N S 1 D f g
Subtraho, xi, ēre, V A. 3 Conj ex fub &
   traho
Succedo, ffi ēre V N 3 Conj er fub & cedo
Succenfeo, ūi, ēre, V N 2 Conj ex fub & cen
   feo
Sufficio, ēci, ēre V N 3 Conj ex fub & ficio.
Suffitus, ûs, N S. 4 D m g
Su, fron Prim
Sum, fui, effe, V N.
Summus, a, um, N A 3 Term superl. a super.
Superba, æ, N S 1 D f g
Superbus a, um, N A. 3 Term.

Superficies, ei, N. S. D f g.

Superior oris N A 3 A.

Supero, āvi, āre, V A 1 Conj

Superfedeo, edi, ēre, V N 2 Conj ex super &
    fedeo

Supplicatio, onis, N S. 3 D f g

Suppeditor, a us fum, ari, V P 1 Conj

Surgens, tis, Part Præf a furgo

Surgo, rexi, ere, V. A. 3 Conj. ex fub &
    rego

Sufpiro, āvi, āre, V. N 1 Conj ex fub &
    fpiro

Suftento, āvi, āre, V. A 1 Conj

Suftentor atus fum, āri, V P 1 Conj.

Sufurro, ōnis, N S. 3 D m g.

Suus, fua, fuum, Pron.

T.

TAbula, æ, N. S. 1 D f g.
    Tædet, V Imp. 2 Conj.

Tardus, a, um, N A 3 Term.

Tectum, i, N S 2 D. n g.

Tego, xi, ěre, V A 3 Conj

Tegor, ctus fum, gi, V. P 3 Conj.

Tellus, ūris. N S 3 D. f g

Tempus, ŏris, N. S 3 D n g

Tenacula, æ, N S 1 D f g.

Tendo tětendi, ěre, V A 3 Conj

Tenebræ, arum, N S 1 D f g

Teneo, ui, ere, V A 2 Conj

Teneor, ten tus fum, teneri, V P 2 Conj.

Tentorium, i, N S. 2 D. n g

Tenuis, is, N A 3 Ait

Tergiverfator, ōris, N. S 3 D. m g.

Tergum, i, N S 2 D n g

Terminus, i, N S. 2 D. m g.

Terra,

Terra, æ, N S 1 D f g
Testa, æ, N S 1 D f g
Testimonium, ii, N S 2 D. n g.
Testis, is, N S 3 D c g
Testor atus sum, āri, V D 1 Conj
Thesaurus, 1, N S 2 D m g
Timens, tis, Part Præf a timeo.
Timeo, ūi, ēre, V N 2 Conj
Timor, ōris, N S 3 D m g
Titubo, āvi, are, V N 1 Conj.
Torrens, tis N S 3 D m g
Totus a um, N A 3 Term
Tracto, āvi a e, V A 1 Conj
Trado, dĭdi, ere, V. A. 3 Conj ex trans & do.
Tranquillitas, ātis N S 3 D f g
Tranquillus, a, um N A 3 Term
Transeo īvi, ii, ire V N 4 Conj ex trans & eo.
Transfossio, ōnis, N S 3 D f g
Transgrediens, tis Part Præf a transgredior.
Tremor, ōris, N S 3 D m g
Tres, trium, N A 3 Art
Tributarius, ii, N S 2 D. m g
Triplicatus, a um, Part Præt a triplicor.
Tristitia, æ, N S 1 D f g
Tristis, is, N A 3 Art
Triticum, 1, N S 2 D n g
Trutina, æ, N S 1 D f, g.
Tu, Pron Prim
Tumultuosus, a, um, N A. 3 Term.
Turbo, īnis, N S. 3 D f g
Turbo, āvi, a e V A 1 Conj
Turris, is, N S 3 D f g
Tutus, a, um, N A 3 Term
Tuus, a, um, N A. 3 Term

V. Vagor,

V.

Vagor, ātus fum, āri, V D. 1 Conj
 Vallis, is, N S 3 D f g.
Vallus, a um, N A 3 Term
Vanitas, atis N S 3 D f g
Vanus, a um N A 3 Term
Vapor, oris, N S 3 D m g
Varius, a, um, N A 3 Term
Vas, sis, N S 3 D n g
Vastatio, ōnis, N S 3 D f g
Vastitas, atis, N S 3 D f g
Vectis, is, N S. 3 D m. g
Vehemens, tis, N A 3 Art.
Vendens, tis, Part Præs a vendo.
Vendo, didi, ěre, V A 3 Conj
Venio, veni ire, V N 4 Conj
Venor, atus fum, ari V D 1 Conj
Venter, tris, N S 3 D m g
Vento, avi are, V A 1 Conj
Ventus, i, N S 2 D m g
Verax, ācis, N A 3 Art
Verbum i, N S 2 D n g
Veritas, itis, N S 3 D f g
Versor, ātus fum, āri, V D 1 Conj.
Versutus, a, um N A 3 Term
Vertigus, i, N S 2 D m. g
Verto, ti, ěre, V A 3 Conj
Verus, a, um, N A 3 Term.
Vesber, i, N S 2 D m g
Vestimentum, i, N S 2 D m g.
Vestis, is, N S 3 D f. g
Vexatio, ōnis, N S 3 D f g
Via, æ, N S 1 D f g
Victor ōris, N S 3 D m g
Vicinus, i, N S 2 D m g.
Videns, tis, Part Præs a video.

Video,

Video, di, t.e V A. 2 Conj

Videor, visus sum, ēri, V P 2 Conj.

Vidua, æ, N S 1 D f g

Vincor, victus sum, vinci, V P 3 Con)

Vinea æ, N. S 1 D f g

Vinosus ı um N A. 3 Term.

Vinum ı, N S 2 D n g,

Violentia, æ N S 1 D f g

Violentus, ı, um, N A 3 Term

Vir, viri, N S 2 D m g

Virga, æ, N S 1 D f g

Virtus, ūtis, N S 3 D f g

Vis vin, v', N S 3 D f g

Visio, ōnis N S 3 D f g

Visitor, ōris N S 3 D m g

Visitor, atus sum, ari V P 1 Conj

Vita, æ, N S 1 D f g

Vivens, tis, Part, Præf a vivo

Vivo, xi, ĕre, V N 3 Conj.

Vivus, a, um, N A 3 Term

Ultimus, a, um, N A Sup ıb ultra.

Umbra, æ N S 1 D f g

Unguentum, ı, N S 2 D n g

Uaus, a, um, N A 3 Term

Unusquisque, N A 3 Term. ex unus & quisq

Voco avi, āre, V A 1 Conj

Vocor, atus sum, āri, V P. 1 Conj

Vola, æ, N S 1 D f. g

Volito, āvi, are, V N 1 Conj

Volo, lui, velle, V Irr

Voluntis, atis, N S. 3 D f g.

Voluptas, ytis, N S 3 Conj

Vomitus, ûs, N S 4 D m g

Vorator, ōris, N S 3 D m g.

Voveo, vi, ēre, V N 2 Conj.

Vox, vocis, N, S 3 D f g.

Urbs, bis, N. S 3 D f g.

Uro.

Uro ffi, ĕre, v. A 3 Conj.

Urſa, æ, N S 1 D f g

Urſus, i, N S 2 D m g

Urtica, æ N S 1 D f g

Uter, utra, utrum, N A 3 Term.

Uterque, traque, trumque, N A 3 Term.

Uterus, i, N 2 D m g

Utor, uſus ſum, ti, V D 3 Conj.

Vulnus, ĕris, N S. 3 D n g.

Vultus, ûs, N. S 4 D m. g.

FINIS.

Lightning Source UK Ltd.
Milton Keynes UK
UKHW030643070223
416609UK00013B/2953

9 781170 333112